Motivating EFL Learners with Authentic Materials

英語学習者のモチベーションを高めるための授業実践とその効果
オーセンティックな教材を用いて

林　千代　Chiyo HAYASHI

溪水社

まえがき

　本書の目的は、外国語学習者のモチベーションを高めることを目的として行われた授業実践および実証的研究について、研究成果を報告することである。近年、第二言語・外国語教育において、モチベーション（motivation）、ビリーフ（beliefs）、不安（anxiety）、自己調整力（self-regulation）、自己肯定感（self-efficacy）など、学習者の様々な個人差要因（individual differences）が言語習得に及ぼす影響について、研究が盛んに行われている。その中でもモチベーションは特に注目を浴びており、どのような言語教授法・教材・授業デザインがモチベーションを高める効果があるかについて、関心が高まっている。しかし、具体的にどのような教授法や教材がモチベーションを高めるかについては、未だに十分な研究が行われているとは言えない。そこで、本書ではモチベーションを高めることを目的に行われた「英語授業実践」について詳細を述べ、その成果を実証的に検証した結果について報告する。

　学習者のモチベーション・学習意欲を高めることは、教育の場における重要なテーマである。近年、教育学、心理学をはじめ、広い分野でモチベーションについて研究が行われている。このように、モチベーションが重要視されるのは、大きく二つの理由がある。まず、学習者のモチベーションは、学習意欲および学習行動と密接に関わっているからである。つまり、「学びへのモチベーション」が高まることにより、学習者が自ら意欲的に学習に取り組み、集中した学習を継続することが可能となる。その結果、学習の効果が高まり、学習者はより深く学び、多くの学習成果を達成することができるのである。

　もう一つの理由は、モチベーションの特性に関わっている。様々な個人差要因の中でも、性格・気質などは恒常的であり、比較的変化しにくいとされている。しかし、モチベーションは、学習者が置かれた環境や状況、例えば授業や

教員の指導などにより、変化しやすいとされている。つまり、学習者それぞれに相応しく、効果的な指導を行えば、学習へのモチベーションが高まる可能性が高いということである。これらの 2 つの点、モチベーションと学習成果の密接なつながり、そして教育効果が表れやすい点が、モチベーション研究が盛んにおこなわれている理由であると考えられる。

　本書が理論的基盤としているのは、アメリカの心理学者である Edward L. Deci と Richard M. Ryan が提唱している自己決定理論（Self-determination theory、以後 SDT）である。SDT（Deci & Ryan, 2000）とは、さまざまな領域における動機づけをとらえる包括的な理論的枠組みであり、外国語教授法研究においても、多くの研究者がこの理論を研究の拠り所としている。SDT の根本にあるのは、自己決定の重要さ、つまり、学習者自らが決めるという「自己決定」の度合いが大きければ大きいほど、動機づけも大きくなるという理論である。SDT の特徴の一つは、外発的動機づけを自己決定の度合いにより、いくつかに細分化し、内発的動機付けにつながる連続体としてとらえていることである。

　SDT は内発的動機づけ（intrinsic motivation）が高まる前提条件として、3 つの心理的欲求が満たされることを想定している。「自律性（autonomy）の欲求」は、自分の行動を自分がコントロールしているという実感であり、「有能性（Competence）の欲求」は行動をやり遂げる自信や自己の能力を示したいという欲求、「関係性（relatedness）の欲求」は周囲の人々や社会と密接なつながりをもち、他者と友好的な関係性を築きたいという欲求である。SDT によると、これらの 3 つの欲求が満たされた結果、学習者は内発的に動機づけられ、学習にも自律的に取り組むようになるとしている。

　本研究が「外国語教授法」の理論的枠組みとして参照したのは、「内容重視教育法」（content-based instruction、以後 CBI）である。CBI は、近年 CLIL（content and language integrated instruction）と同様に注目を浴びている言語教育のアプローチである。CBI には大きく 2 つの目標があり、「外国語の習得」と

まえがき

その外国語を使って教える「教科内容の習得」を目指す。例えば、「英語で行う歴史の授業」や「音楽を英語で教える授業」が挙げられる。

　上記のモチベーション理論と外国語教授法に基づいて、学習者のモチベーションを高めるために、4種類の統合的な授業をデザインし、その効果をそれぞれ実証的に検証した。自己決定理論に基づいて、「自律性（autonomy）の欲求」、「有能性（Competence）の欲求」、「関係性（relatedness）の欲求」を満たす指導法・アクティビティを取り入れ、内容重視教育法の枠組みに沿って、オーセンティックな教材（コンテント）を取り入れた授業実践を行った。

　本書では、これらの実践・研究の詳細と結果について報告する。本書の構成は次のとおりである。第1章「序論」では研究の概観を短くまとめた論文を紹介し、第2章では研究の理論的背景とTED Talksを用いた授業実践研究、第3章では、英語で書かれた歌を教材として用いた実践、第4章では英語で書かれた絵本・児童文学を扱った事例研究を報告する。最後に、第5章では、日本人学習者が授業内での「チョイス」、つまり学生が「自分で選ぶこと」をどのようにとらえているかについて調査した研究結果について報告する。

　本書は、著者が2013年から2018年の間に発表した論文に加筆・修正を加えたものを一冊にまとめたものである。使用する言語は、オリジナルの論文のままとし、第1章は日本語、第2章以降は英語とする。

　本書の刊行は多くの方のサポートを得ることにより、可能になった。ご指導、ご支援くださった方々、また参加者である学生に深く謝意を表したい。また、本書の出版をお引き受けいただき、刊行にご尽力いただいた渓水社の木村斉子氏、宇津宮沙紀氏に心から感謝の気持ちを表する。

　本書は、文部科学省科学研究費補助金（JP15K02692）を得て刊行した。

2019年2月28日　　　　　　　　　　　　　　　　　　　　　　　　　　著者

目次

まえがき i

CHAPTER 1
序章：研究の概観
オーセンティックな教材を用いた統合的な英語授業実践

1. 研究目的 3
2. モチベーションの重要性 3
3. 自己決定理論 3
4. 動機付けが高まる条件 4
5. 動機付けを高めるための英語授業デザイン 5
    5.1 方法　5
    5.2 授業実践　5
    5.3 結果と考察　6
    5.4 結論と示唆　7

CHAPTER 2
Motivating EFL Learners through TED Talks
TED Talksを使ったモチベーションを高めるための英語授業

1. Introduction 9
2. Motivation in Language Learning 10
3. A Self-Determination Approach to Motivation 11
4. Content-Based Instruction (CBI) 15
5. Objective of the Study 17
6. Method 18
    6.1 Participants　18
    6.2 Research Design　18

    6.3 Instruments of the Study   19
7. Content-Based Instruction with TED Talks on Music 20
8. Teaching Procedures 22
9. Data Collection and Analyses 23
10. Results and Discussion 23
11. Conclusion 28

CHAPTER 3
Using Songs in EFL Classrooms
英語の歌を教材として使用した内容重視型授業

1. Introduction 31
2. Content-Based Language Instruction (CBI) 32
3. The Study 34
4. Method 35

    4.1 Participants   35

    4.2 Instrument of the Study   35

5. Content-Based Intervention 35

    5.1 Phase 1: Studying English Songs   36

    5.2 Phase 2: "My Favorite Song" Presentation   38

6. Students' Perceptions of the Content-Based Instruction with Songs 40
7. Conclusion 43

CHAPTER 4
Using Children's Literature in EFL Classrooms
絵本・児童文学を使用した英語授業

1. Introduction 45
2. Children's Literature in Adult Education 46
3. Special Features of Children's Books for Adult Language Learners 48
4. Criteria for Book Selection 51

5. Teaching Children's Literature in the L2 College Classroom 52
    5.1 Context of Teaching　52
    5.2 Teaching Procedures　53
    5.3 Book Selection Criteria　54
    5.4 Picture Books, Synopses, Students' Reactions　54
    5.5 Students' Perceptions of Reading Picture Books　56
6. Conclusion 58

CHAPTER 5
"Choice" in EFL Classrooms
英語の授業における「チョイス」

1. Introduction 62
2. Literature Review 62
    2.1 Self-Determination Theory　62
    2.2 Autonomy Support in Classrooms　64
    2.3 Choice and Intrinsic Motivation　65
    2.4 Cross-Cultural Views on Autonomy and Choice　66
    2.5 Studies on Choice　67
3. Purpose of the Study 68
4. Method 68
    4.1 Participants and Instrument　68
    4.2 Project: "Talk Like a TED Speaker"　69
5. Results and Discussion 71
    5.1 Topics Students Chose　71
    5.2 Questionnaire Results　74
6. Conclusion 77

索引 81

英語学習者のモチベーションを高めるための
授業実践とその効果
――オーセンティックな教材を用いて――

Motivating EFL Learners with Authentic Materials

CHAPTER 1
序章：研究の概観
オーセンティックな教材を用いた統合的な英語授業実践

1. 研究目的
　本章では、英語学習に対するモチベーションを高める目的で行った「オーセンティックな教材を用いた統合的な英語授業」の実践内容及びその効果について、概観を報告するものである。研究の理論的な背景は、「自己決定理論」に依拠し、学習者の心理的ニーズ（有能性、自律性、関係性）を高めるべくデザインした授業を行い、質問紙調査（量的・質的）にて授業効果を実証的に検証した。

2. モチベーションの重要性
　学習者一人一人の学習におけるモチベーション、つまり動機づけの重要性は広く認識されており、第2言語・外国語学習においても、学習者の動機付けは、最重要な課題となっている。近年、教育の現場において学習者の多様な意欲や動機付けを解明するために、「自己決定理論」（self-determination theory）（Ryan & Deci, 2000）が包括的な枠組みを提供している。この理論の出発点は、「人はみな自分自身の行動の源泉でありたい」という人間の根本的な心理的欲求であり、自分の行動を外的な要因により強制されるのではなく、自らの自己決定により選択したいという普遍的な人間の心理を前提としている。

3. 自己決定理論
　自己決定理論は、動機付けを大きく「内から湧き上がるもの」（内発的）（intrinsic）と「外部からの刺激・環境によるもの」（外発的）（extrinsic）動機付けに区分し、外発的動機付けは自己決定の度合いが異なる複数の要因か

ら成り立つ「有機的な連続体」としてとらえている。自ら決定した度合いが高いものから順に、統合的（integrated）調整、同一化（identified）調整、取り入れ的（introjected）調整、外的（external）調整としている。

　内発的な動機づけは、「楽しい・興味がある・夢中になる」という学習者の内部から湧き上がるもっとも自律的な動機づけであり、豊かな経験、深い理解、高い創造性、効果的な問題解決を導き出す。一方、外発的動機付けは、「義務・報酬・賞罰」などの学習者に内在しない外側からの動機づけを意味する。外的動機づけの中には、外的な価値を自ら取り入れることにより、内在化が進み、自ら自分のために行う行動、つまり「自己決定的」になる場合もあるとされている。

4. 動機付けが高まる条件

　教育の現場で学習者の動機付けを高めるには、どのような授業が必要なのであろうか。自己決定理論によると。学習者に内在する3つの心理的欲求を満たすことで、内発的動機づけが高まるとしている。それらは、（1）自律性（autonomy）：自分自身の決定で行動したいという欲求、（2）有能性（competence）：自ら望む結果を達成するための自信や自分の能力を示したいという欲求、（3）関係性（relatedness）：周りの人と密接に関わり合い友好的な関係を築きたい欲求、の3種類である。これらを満たす具体的な授業方略としては、具体的には（1）学習者が興味を持つトピック・コンテンツの導入、学生の意見を取りいれ、学生自ら選択できる機会の提供（自律性）、（2）基本語彙・文法の復習をしながら、理解可能なインプットの提供、学生が達成感を感じることができるような足場架け、自己肯定感につながる評価（有能性）、（3）学生が友好的な関係を育むことのできる環境作り、自分のアイデンティティのもとに「本物の会話」をする状況作り（Ushioda, 2011）（関係性）、などが挙げられるであろう。

5. 動機付けを高めるための英語授業デザイン

上記の動機づけニーズを高めるべくデザインされた英語授業を、異なる学生を対象に2種類（Study 1、Study 2）試みた。言語教授法は、内容重視教授法（content-based instruction）とコミュニカティブ・ランゲージ・ティーチングに依拠し、それぞれ異なるオーセンティックな教材を用いた。それぞれの授業効果を質問紙を用いて量的・質的に検証した。

5.1 方法

自己決定理論による3つの動機づけニーズを高めるべくデザインされた「統合的な教育的介入」を試みた。Study 1では52名（初級: 英検3級〜準2級）、Study 2では90名（中級: 英検準2級〜2級）の音楽専攻の大学生が参加した。いずれも著者が担当した必修英語授業の受講者である。英語学習に対する動機づけの変化を縦断的に調査するために、30項目からなる質問紙調査（4件法）（表1）を教育的介入前後に2回行なった。

表1

英語学習動機づけ尺度の要因と項目例

動機付け要因	質問項目例（英語を学ぶ理由）
内発的動機付け	英語を学ぶのは楽しいから
同一化調整	自分の成長に役に立つから
取り入れ調整	勉強しないと気まずいから
外的調整	よい成績を取りたいから
無動機	英語を学ぶのは無駄だと思う

注. 質問紙はHiromori（2006）を参照した。

5.2 授業実践

上記の3欲求を満たすべく、Study 1・Study 2ともに、以下に挙げる4つの柱を取り入れた統合的授業を10週間実践した。

①Small Talk: 英語が話せるという自信を育て、学びのコミュニティーと「本物の会話」ができる状況作りのために、学生が普段日本語で行う会話を想定した

質問リストを英語で作成（質問項目は学生からのインプット）。毎回、学生はこのリストを見ながら、10分間日常・大学生活について英語のみで会話。
②音楽に関するコンテント：学生が音楽専攻であることから、インターネットから音楽に関するオーセンティックな題材を教材として導入。Study 1では英語の歌（YouTubeから "When you wish upon a star" など）、Study 2では音楽に関するTED Talks（"Transformative power of music"など）を選び、ワークシートを作成して授業。
③英語基礎力強化：テキストを用いて、基本文法・語彙の復習。
④プレゼンテーション：Study 1では "My favorite song" を自分で選び、スライド作成・発表、Study 2では "Talk like a TED speaker" と題し、自分が興味・関心を持っているトピックを自ら選んで、スライドを作成・発表。
(タイムラインは、第1週～6週までは①、②、③、第7週～8週は④の準備、第9週～10週で④を行った。)

5.3 結果と考察

　動機付け質問紙調査（4件法）を2回（4月と7月）実施した結果、Study 1（$N = 52$）では、内発的動機付けは、4月は、$M = 2.50$、$SD = .60$であったが、7月は、$M = 2.80$、$SD = .69$であった。被験者間で4月と7月の内発的動機付けに差があるかどうかについてt検定を行ったところ、有意差が見られた（$t(51) = 3.66, p < .01$）。Study 2（$N = 90$）でも同様の分析を行った。4月は、$M = 2.80$、$SD = .58$、7月は$M = 2.95$、$SD = .56$、t検定を行ったところ、有意差が見られた（$t(89) = -2.96, p < .01$）。学生の記述調査では、「small talkを毎回することにより、自分でも英語が話せるという自信がついた」、「英語を勉強だけでとらえるのではなく、好きな音楽と一緒に学べて興味・関心が湧いた」、「自分でも英語の歌・TED Talksを聞いて、英語の勉強を始めた」など、自らの英語力に対して肯定的になり、自律的な学びへと繋がる記述がみられた。本研究のためにデザインされた統合的な授業が内発的動機付けの向上に効果的であったと思われる。

5.4 結論と示唆

　本研究では、SDTの枠組みに基づいて、3つの心理的なニーズを満たす教育介入を行った結果、内発的動機付けが高まったことが明らかになった。授業を統合的にデザインし、自分のアイデンティティのもとに「本物の会話」をする活動、学習者にとって興味深いコンテント（教材）、学習者が自ら決定できる機会、などを授業に組み込むことが、内発的動機付けの向上に繋がったと考えられる。今後の研究としては、動機づけにおける学生の「個人差要因」をさらに深く理解するために、インタビューなどの質的な調査も行う必要がある。また、高まった自律性がその後どのように自己調整力へと繋がるかについてもさらなる研究が必要である。

References

Hiromori, T. (2006). The effects of educational intervention on l2 learners' motivational development. *JACET Bulletin, 43*, 1-14.

Ryan, R. M., & Deci, E. L. (2000). Self-determination theory and the facilitation of intrinsic motivation, social development, and well-being. *American Psychologist, 55*, 68-78.

Ushioda, E. (2011) Motivating learners to speak as themselves. In G. Murray, X. Gao, & T. Lamb (Eds.), *Identity, motivation and autonomy in language learning* (pp. 11-24). Bristol: Multilingual Matters.

［本章は、「英語教育」（大修館、2017年11月号）に掲載された原稿に若干手を加えたものです。］

CHAPTER 2
Motivating EFL Learners through TED Talks
TED Talks を使ったモチベーションを高めるための英語授業

【概要】

　本章は、大学生を対象として、英語学習に対するモチベーションを高めるために行った縦断的な英語教育実践について報告する。理論的な背景は「自己決定理論」に依拠し、言語教授法としては、「内容重視教育法」を用いた。教材としては、オーセンティックな教材として TED Talks（音楽に関する内容）を使用した。自己決定理論に基づいた質問紙を用い、学生のモチベーションの変化を二学期間にわたって調査した結果、内発的動機が有意に向上したことが明らかになった。また、学生の自由記述を分析した結果、多くの学生は、「TED Talks の内容が興味深かった」、「楽しく自然に英語が学べた」と記述していた。少数であるが、教室外でも自分で TED Talks を聞き英語を学ぶ自律した学習者になった学生もいた。しかし、同時に、英語が早すぎてわかりにくいなどの記述も見られ、学生の理解度を高めるためには、さらなる足場架けも必要であることが明らかになった。また、内容としては、音楽専攻学生を対象に行った授業であったので、音楽に関する TED Talks を選んだが、音楽以外の内容を学びたいと述べた学生もいたため、学生の多様な興味と関心に応えることも必要であることがわかった。

Keywords: content-based instruction, authentic materials, motivation

1. Introduction

　　The current study reports on a content-based teaching practice which aimed at enhancing motivation for studying English through the use of TED Talks. The theoretical background of the study is self-determination theory (SDT) (Deci & Ryan, 1985, 2002), which represents a broad framework that explains human behaviour and motivation. In addition, this practice was guided by content-based language instruction (CBI), a holistic approach to language teaching, designed to merge language and content instruction (Brinton, Snow, & Wesche, 1989).

2. Motivation in Language Learning

Motivation plays an important role in education because it generally explains why people do something, how much effort they exert when they pursue goals, and how long they persist in engaging in the action (Dörnyei, 2001). It has been well-acknowledged that motivation plays a critical role in learning because higher motivation leads to deeper engagement (Noels, 2001). In second language (L2) learning contexts, motivation has been widely acknowledged as one of the key factors in achieving not only a high level of proficiency but also deeper learning of the content being taught (Noels, Pelletier, Clément, & Vallerand, 2003). In short, L2 learning motivation is one of the most influential factors that influence the depth and quality of learning (Lasagabaster, 2011).

L2 motivation research started with Gardner and Lambert (1959, 1972). They suggested that learners' motivation for studying a second language consists of two types of orientations: the integrative and the instrumental. The former refers to a desire to learn a second language in order to be integrated in the society where the language is spoken. For instance, L2 learners may wish to be liked and accepted by the people in the L2 community. This personalized, interpersonal desire is reflected in the integrative orientation (Gardner & Lambert, 1972). The latter, on the other hand, refers to a utilitarian desire to learn a language because the language skills are useful and valuable tools that enable people to achieve better life outcomes, such as getting a better paying job, entering a good school, gaining higher social recognition or higher self-esteem, or traveling in foreign countries.

Of these two orientations, Gardner and Lambert (1972) have indicated that the integrative orientation is more closely associated with successful language learning. However, studies conducted in English as a foreign language (EFL) contexts have shown that the instrumental orientation is more influential than the integrated orientation in countries where the target language is rarely used in daily life (Lukmani, 1972). Accordingly, Clément and Kruidenier (1983) suggested that it was necessary to consider the influence of the social milieu because they found that the integrative orientation appeared only in multicultural contexts among members of a clearly dominant group.

In recent years, with the radical changes that have been taking place in the world, Ushioda (2011) pointed out the weakening role of the integrative orientation: "Traditional concepts such as integrative motivation lose their explanatory power when English is becoming a 'must-have' basic educational skill and when there is no clearly defined target language community" (p. 199). One of the possible reasons for this change can be attributed to the acceleration of the globalization, which has made English as a lingua franca that enables people in different nations to communicate with each other despite the differences in their first languages.

3. A Self-Determination Approach to Motivation

In educational psychology, many theories of motivation (e.g., expectancy-value theory by Eccles & Wigfield, 2002; self-efficacy theory by Bandura, 1986; and self-determination theory by Deci & Ryan, 1985) have emerged to better understand learners in diverse educational contexts. Of these theories, self-determination theory (SDT) has been referred to as one of the most reliable frameworks to understand L2 learners' motivation for learning a language (Hiromori, 2006). This theory addresses social-contextual conditions that promote versus hinder the natural processes of self-motivation and healthy psychological development (Deci & Ryan, 1985; Ryan & Deci, 2000). The central tenet of this theory is the distinction between two types of behaviors: one that emanates from one's sense of self and the other that stems from outside of one's self. The former represents intrinsically motivated behaviors that are performed out of interest and curiosity, thereby satisfying an individual's innate psychological needs for competence and autonomy. On the other hand, behaviour that stems from outside of one's self represents extrinsically motivated behaviors that are performed due to outside pressure or control. This distinction can be explained using the notion, the locus of causality. When a behaviour is determined by one's self, the locus of causality is internal to one's self; therefore, the regulatory process involves "choice". However, when a behaviour is controlled by outside factors, the locus of causality is external to the self; therefore, the regulatory process involves *compliance* (Deci, Vallerand, Pelletier, & Ryan, 1991, p. 327). Basic tenets of these two motivations are briefly explained below.

Intrinsic motivation is defined as "the doing of an activity for its inherent satisfactions rather than for some separable consequence" (Ryan & Deci, 2000, p. 56). When intrinsically motivated, a person is spontaneously moved to act for the fun or challenge that accompanies the given task. For example, when people become absorbed in reading a mystery just for the fun of it, they are intrinsically motivated to read because they engage in the act of reading based on an inner desire to do so. Another common example is from the realm of music; if people play a musical instrument because of the sense of enjoyment they experience, they are intrinsically motivated.

This focus on intrinsic motivation within SDT is explained by a sub-theory known as cognitive evaluation theory (CET) (Deci & Ryan, 1985; Ryan & Deci, 2000). CET suggests that social environments can facilitate or forestall intrinsic motivation by supporting versus blocking people's fulfillment of their psychological needs. Based on the findings of empirical research, CET is focused primarily on three psychological needs, "competence, autonomy, and relatedness, which, when satisfied, yield enhanced self-motivation and mental health and, when prevented, lead to decreased motivation and self-being" (Ryan & Deci, 2000, p. 68). Competence is defined as one's perceived abilities in performing given tasks and "being efficacious in performing the requisite actions". Relatedness is defined as "developing secure and satisfying connections with others in one's social environment". Autonomy is as "being self-initiating and self-regulating of one's own actions" (Deci, Vallerand, Pelletier, and Ryan, 1991, p. 327). CET posits that these three factors are essential for positive behaviors and the enhancement of intrinsic motivation, which result in high-quality learning and creativity (Ryan & Deci, 2000).

Extrinsic motivation, on the other hand, refers to behaviors that are considered a means to an end (Deci & Ryan, 1985). In other words, extrinsically motivated behaviors are instrumental in nature because they are performed not out of a deep-seated interest in the activity, but to attain some separable outcomes. For instance, if students do their homework to avoid being scolded by their teachers, their actions are extrinsically motivated because they engage in the activity to avoid punishment. Or if they study English to pass an entrance examination, they are extrinsically motivated because their action is driven by the desire to attain the separable outcome of passing the test.

Deci and Ryan (1985) identified four types of extrinsically motivated behaviors, and proposed a second sub-theory, organismic integration theory

(OIT). This theory classifies extrinsic motivation into four types: external, introjected, identified, and integrated forms of regulation. The least self-determined behaviors are referred to as external regulation. Such behaviors are performed to satisfy external demands or to receive rewards, not out of interest in the activity. The locus of control is outside of the person. Thus, if children stop playing a video game because they are afraid of being scolded by their parents, they are externally regulated. A second type of extrinsic motivation is introjected regulation, which involves following a regulation but not fully accepting it as one's own decision. If students submit homework on time because they do not want to be regarded as lazy, their action reflects introjected regulation, or "internal coercion" (Deci, Vallerand, Pelletier, & Ryan, 1991, p. 329). The locus of control is somewhat external, and behaviors are performed to avoid guilt or anxiety. A more autonomous type of motivation is identified regulation. This occurs when individuals have come to value the behavior and have accepted it as "personally important" (Ryan & Deci, 2000). If students do extra work outside of the classroom because they believe it will help them improve their performance at school, this attitude shows identified regulation. This behaviour is still externally regulated because it is performed primarily because of its usefulness or instrumentality for the goal of improving school grades, and not because of interest or enjoyment. The least controlled form of motivation is integrated regulation. Integrated regulation occurs when "identified regulations have been fully assimilated by the self" (Ryan & Deci, 2000, p. 62). That is, people integrate the value of the behaviour into "their own self-schemas and engage in behaviour because of its importance to their senses of self" (Schunk, Pintrich, & Meece, 2008, p. 243). For example, when people exercise regularly to improve their health, this behavior reflects integrated regulation in that this action is internally regulated because of its own value. That is, they exercise not because it is inherently fun, but because they know that exercise will help them live a healthier life. Although integrated regulation shares many qualities with intrinsic motivation, there is one distinct difference: the former is carried out to achieve a separable outcome beyond performing the action itself, but the latter is done for the inherent satisfaction gained from performing the action.

As discussed above, self-determination theory makes a critical distinction between intrinsic and extrinsic motivation: volitional behaviors that emanate from one's sense of self and those performed because of outside pressure or control. This theory postulates that promoting greater self-determination is an important developmental goal. Furthermore, it posits that support for learners' feeling of competence, autonomy, and relatedness is essential for human development (Ryan & Deci, 2000).

4. Content-Based Instruction (CBI)

During the last decade, there has been a sharp rise in interest in an integrated instruction which combines content and language instruction, namely, content and language integrated instruction (CLIL) or content-based instruction (CBI). CBI is one approach to language teaching that focuses not only on the language itself but also on what is being taught through the language. This approach views the target language as "the vehicle through which a specific type of content is learned" rather than as the immediate object of the study (Brinton, Snow, & Wesche, 1989, p.5). Thus, in a CBI class, the goals are twofold: learning about the content and the language. For example, Japanese college students who major in business may study *Business Management* with materials written in English and use English as the tool of communication both in writing and speaking. Or students may learn about endangered animals in a required college English class, using articles or videos from the National Geography website.

The content of CBI instruction can be diverse and flexible (Genesee, 1994). Curtain and Pesola (1994) suggests that the content should be related to curriculum concepts being taught through the language, such as history, science, and math. Genesee (1994) points out that the content can be non-academic matters as long as it is interesting and important for the learner. Met (1991) states that the content should be materials which are cognitively engaging and demanding for the learner. Despite these differences in the conception of the topics, perhaps, it is best to choose a subject or topic which is most suitable for learners, considering not only the curriculum goals but also students' interests and future needs.

There are other effective instructional approaches that have been incorporated into CBI instruction: cooperative learning, learning strategy instruction, and extensive reading (Grabe & Stroller, 1997). Thus, it is possible to view CBI as an integrated instructional method based on extensive research outcomes in second language acquisition (SLA) and educational psychology. According to Brinton, Snow, and Wesche (1989), the advantages of CBI can be summed up as follows: a) students are able to learn a specific subject matter through the use of the target language; b) the integration of the four traditional language skills; c) the use of authentic materials; d) discussion of materials; e) academic writing which enables students to synthesize facts and ideas from multiple sources; and e) the actual use of a variety of language and study skills (p. 2).

A notable strength of CBI lies in the fact that it can make learning a language more motivating and engaging since interesting and stimulating content can be brought into regular language classrooms. A specific type of new knowledge is learned through the use of the language, which can make students both more confident and independent. When students have high interest in the content being taught, it is natural for them to become more tedengaged in learning about the content.

Grabe and Stroller (1997) stated "interest in content information, and the successes students attribute to content learning, can lead to powerful intrinsic motivation" (p. 12). Intrinsic motivation may lead to "flow", the state of deep engagement when personal skills are matched by high challenge: the total absorption in the activity and a sense of timelessness (Csikszentmihalyi, 1990).

Despite these advantages, it is necessary to recognize some difficulties in practicing CBI in language classrooms. Because CBI is not explicitly focused on language learning, less proficient students may need more linguistic support. CBI often uses authentic materials which tend to be challenging in terms of vocabulary, syntactic complexity, and sentence length; therefore, care should be taken in order to make the materials more approachable and comprehensible. Furthermore, because it is not easy for such learners to communicate in the target language, it is necessary to provide linguistic support for output by providing a list of useful vocabulary and phrases for speaking and writing.

While content-based instruction can be challenging for less proficient L2 learners, it is an effective method which efficiently merges language and content learning. The merits of CBI include increased use of the target language, integration of the four language skills, and development of academic skills and content knowledge. In particular, CBI can potentially enhance motivation and desire for learning interesting content.

5. Objective of the Study

The current study aims at investigating the longitudinal effects of a content-based intervention on Japanese college students' motivation for learning English. Self-determination theory (SDT) is referred to as the theory of motivation that guides the study, and content-based instruction

(CBI) is the approach for teaching. Music was chosen as the content of the intervention because the participants were music majors. The research questions were posed as follows:

1. How does the content-based instruction with TED Talks (about music) impact Japanese college students' motivation for learning English?
2. How did the students perceive the intervention?

6. Method
6.1 Participants

The participants of the current study are 90 first- and second-year music majors attending a private music college in Tokyo. They were enrolled in a required two-semester English class that met twice a week for 90 minutes. The participants were divided into six different classes in three different proficiency levels (2 low classes, 2 middle classes, and 2 high classes) by the Eiken placement test scores. The students' proficiency ranged from basic (Eiken 3rd degree) to intermediate (Eiken 2nd degree or above).

6.2 Research Design

Longitudinal motivational changes have been usually examined by panel studies which consist of two or more waves (Ruspini, 2002). The current study adopted a panel study design which consists of three waves. That is, the data with the same subjects were collected three times in one academic school year: Time 1 (in April when the spring semester started), Time 2 (in July when the spring semester was over), and Time 3 (in December when the fall semester was over). Table 1 shows the timeline and the instruments of the study.

Table 1

Research Design

Stages	Week (Semester)	Data Collected
Time 1	Week 1 (spring)	English Learning Motivation (ELM) questionnaire (1st time)
Time 2	Week 14 (spring)	ELM (2nd time)
Time 3	Week 14 (fall)	ELM (3rd time) Course Reflection questionnaire

6.3 Instruments of the Study

The instruments of the study consisted of an English Learning Motivation questionnaire (ELM) based on self-determination theory (Deci & Ryan, 2002) and a reflection questionnaire, which asked the participants to reflect on the class at the end of the academic year. The motivation questionnaire was originally developed and validated by Hiromori (2006). It consisted of five dimensions of motivation (amotivation, external regulation, introjected regulation, identified regulation, and intrinsic regulation), which are ordered in a continuum depending on the degree of self-determination. Although the original questionnaire consisted 18 items (3 or 4 items for each dimension), two to three items were added by the author to include six items for each factor. Thus, in total, there were 30 items, six items for each dimension. Table 2 shows the dimensions and sample items.

Table 2

Motivation Dimensions and Sample Items

Dimensions	Sample Items
Amotivation	"I truly have the impression of wasting time in studying English"
External regulation	"Because I want to get a good grade"
Introjected regulation	"Because I would feel bad about myself if I didn't"
Identified regulation	"Because I think it is good for my personal development"

| Intrinsic motivation | "Because studying English is fun" |

Note. The items were answers to a question, "Why are you studying English?". Responses were collected using a Liker scare 1-4 (1 = strongly disagree, 2 = disagree, 3 = agree, 4 = strongly disagree).

7. Content-Based Instruction with TED Talks on Music

As the content of the instruction, TED talks about music related topics were used. Music was chosen as the content because the participants were music majors who were generally interested in music and had practiced some instruments. This section describes TED Talks, the talks used, and the details of the instruction.

TED (Technology, Entertainment, Design) Talks are broadcast on the Internet by a non-profit organization, under the slogan "Ideas Worth Spreading". Founded in 1984, this organization has offered high quality presentations on diverse topics for free viewing online. Because of easy access and high-quality presentations on a wide range of academic and non-academic topics, TED Talks have been viewed by millions of people around the world. Also, in educational contexts, an increasing number of teachers and educators have used them in their lessons to teach various types of content and skills, including English and presentation skills (Takaesu, 2013).

In the first semester, four TED Talks related to music were chosen as the materials of the class. Table 3 shows the titles of the talks, the synopses and the reasons why they were selected.

Table 3

TED Talks Used in the First Semester

Title (Length)	Synopsis	Reasons for selection
The violin, and my dark night of the soul by Ji-Hae Park	A Korean violinist, Ji-Hae Park talks about how she recovered from depression:	Helps Music majors with suggestions on how to overcome difficult

(12 min. 41 sec.)	it was music through which she was able to lift her out again.	moments in music careers.
Music is medicine by Robert Gupta (9 min. 26 sec.)	Robert Gupta, a violinist with the LA Philharmonic, talks about a violin lesson he once gave to a brilliant, schizophrenic musician and how music was able to heal his mind.	The strong commitment of the speaker to his music career and healing people with it.
Transformative power of music by Benjamin Zander (20 min. 43 sec.)	Benjamin Zander talks about the power of classical music with his own performance. Also, he gives important lessons on life.	Shows how classical music can move people's hearts.
Virtual Choir: 200 voices strong by Eric Whitacre (14 min. 34 sec.)	Eric Whitacre who bled a virtual choir of singers from around the world talks about the creative challenges of making music powered by YouTube.	Shows what music can accomplish with the help of the Internet.

In the second semester, the topics were slightly widened to include presentations which provided useful skills and wisdom for music performance and college life. Table 4 shows the titles, the synopses and the reasons why they were selected.

Table 4
TED Talks Used in the 2nd Semester

Title (Speaker)	Synopsis	Reasons for selection
Try something new for 30 days by Matt Cutts (3 min. 20 sec.)	Matt Cutts suggests trying something we always wanted to do for 30 days.	The talk gives students important lessons on having goals and regulating one's own life to achieve the goals.
Your body language shapes who you are by Amy Cuddy (20 min. 55 sec.)	Social psychologist Amy Cuddy shows how "power posing" helps us feel more confident about ourselves.	Helps students feel more confident when they have to perform in front of a large audience.

How to speak so people want to listen by Julian Treasure (9 min. 54 sec.)	Julian Treasure suggests how to improve our speaking skills from some handy vocal exercises to tips on how to speak with empathy.	Helps students gain better communication and listening skills.
The four ways sound affect us by Julian Treasure (5 min. 46 sec.)	Julian Treasure shows how sound affects us in four significant ways and gives suggestions on how to effectively manage our soundscape.	Shows how our lives are influenced by diverse types of sound and the importance of controlling our sound environment.

8. Teaching Procedures

In a 90-minute class, the TED Talks were taught for about 45 minutes for 12 weeks during the first and second semesters. In principle, the classroom language was English, and authentic communication in English was emphasized. In the lower classes, some Japanese was used to explain difficult vocabulary and concepts. Students studied in groups or pairs to exchange their ideas about the talks. The teacher's role was that of a facilitator who answered questions and gave comments to encourage group/pair interactions.

In class, students studied the talks with a worksheet created by the author. The teaching procedures are shown below:

(1) Pre-watching activities: discuss warm-up questions and check the vocabulary list.
(2) While-watching activities: watch the talk, read subtitles in English or Japanese, and answer comprehension questions.
(3) Post-watching activities: read the transcript of the talk, answer comprehension questions, and check answers in groups.
(4) Reflection activities (assignment): write a summary and a reaction to the talk and share them in groups.

For each talk, the procedures above were repeated with some modifications, depending on the English proficiency of the students. Instruction focused on helping students understand the main idea. As TED Talks tend to be difficult for non-native speakers, special care was given to make them comprehensive. For example, in a class with less proficient students, the main idea was highlighted, read aloud, and translated into Japanese. Or students were encouraged to use Japanese when they discussed their reactions to the talk.

In summary, this instruction with the TED Talks was given to the participants for one academic year (two semesters, 14 weeks each), and its effectiveness was examined by conducting two questionnaires.

9. Data Collection and Analyses

Two instruments described earlier were administered to assess the effectiveness of the TED Talks intervention. First, the English learning Motivation Questionnaire (EML) was administered at three time points: Time 1 (April, the beginning of the spring semester), Time 2 (July, the end of the spring semester), and Time 3 (December, the end of the fall semester). Second, a reflection questionnaire using a Likert-scale and an open-ended format was given at the end of the fall semester.

To analyze the date, first, descriptive statistics were calculated with all the participants, and the differences in the three time points were compared with statistical procedures. Second, the reflections over the intervention were analyzed both quantitatively and qualitatively.

10. Results and Discussion

The aim of the current study was to investigate the effects of a content-based intervention on L2 learners' motivation for learning English with self-determination as its theoretical framework. The results of the study are reported in the order of the research questions.

Research Question 1: What are the longitudinal effects of the content-based intervention on Japanese college learners' motivation for learning English?

In order to answer the first research question, descriptive statistics with all the participants (N = 90) were calculated for each time point. Table 5 shows the means and standard deviations for the five types of motivation at Time 1, Time 2, and Time 3. At Time 1, the highest was Identified (M = 3.32); therefore, participants generally agreed that English was valuable and useful for themselves. The second highest was Intrinsic Motivation (M = 2.80) so the participants were somewhat motivated to learn English. Furthermore, Amotivation was lower than 2 (1.66) so generally speaking, the students regarded English as important and felt that they had to study English because of its usefulness.

Table 5

Changes in Motivation

Motivation Types	Time 1		Time 2		Time 3	
	M	SD	M	SD	M	SD
Intrinsic	2.80	.58	2.91	.58	2.95	.56
Identified	3.32	.58	3.39	.63	3.43	.59
Introjected	2.42	.52	2.44	.54	2.50	.61
External	2.36	.60	2.32	.59	2.40	.64
Amotivation	1.66	.51	1.61	.50	1.54	.48

Note. N = 90. The responses were collected using a Likert scale, 1 = strongly disagree, 2 = disagree, 3 = agree, and 4 = strongly agree.

When the changes in the motivational scale over the three time points (Time 1, Time 2, and Time 3) were compared, it was found that Intrinsic, Identified, Introjected, External increased while Amotivation decreased.

To examine if these changes were statistically significant, a one-way repeated measures ANOVA was conducted. There was a significant effect of the intervention on Intrinsic ($F(2, 178) = 4.46$, $p < .05$). Post hoc tests using Boneferroni correction revealed that the intervention elicited a significant increase in Intrinsic from Time 1 to Time 3. In short, Intrinsic significantly increased while the other changes over the three time points were not significant. In summary, the intervention with the TED talks had a significant effect in fostering intrinsic motivation for learning English although the other types of motivation did not show any statistically significant changes.

In summary, these findings indicated that the intervention with TED Talks had positive effects on L2 learners' motivational development. As the significant increase in intrinsic motivation shows, the participants became more interested in studying English and enjoyed learning it through the TED Talks. This result indicated that the intervention was effective in fostering motivation for learning English.

Research Question 2. How did the students perceive the content-based instruction with the TED Talks about music?

To investigate in detail the participants' perceptions of the intervention with TED Talks, an open-ended questionnaire was administered at the end of the fall semester. Students' responses were coded into distinct categories according to textual content.

The participants' responses showed that they generally perceived the TED Talk intervention positively. Table 6 shows their responses and the number of the students who wrote the responses. Half of the students (48%, $n = 53$) reported that they were able to enjoy learning English because the content of the talks was interesting and enjoyable. A quarter of the students (24%, $n = 24$) mentioned that their English ability improved. About the same number of the students stated that the knowledge which they gained from the talks would be useful in their futures. Other positive responses included learning presentation skills, getting used to native speakers' English and becoming autonomous learners themselves. Finally, it is noteworthy that some stated that studying with TED Talks was more interesting than studying ordinary textbooks. This comment seems to highlight the value of TED Talks as authentic teaching materials. In summary, as these responses indicated, the intervention with the TED talks was effective for getting students more interested in studying English.

Table 6

Students' Positive Responses

	Students' Positive Responses (English translation by the author)	n (%)
1.	内容に興味があり、英語が自然に楽しく学べた。(The talks were interesting, so it was fun to study English with the talks.)	48 (53)
2.	英語のスキルが伸びた（リスニング、語彙、読解など）。(My English skills such as listening, vocabulary, reading skills improved.)	24 (27)
3.	TED Talksから得た知識が自分の生活や将来に役に立つ。(The knowledge I gained from the talks will be useful in my future.)	24 (27)
4.	プレゼンテーションや話し方の勉強になった。(I learned presentation and communication skills.)	14 (16)
5.	ネイティブの自然な英語に慣れることができた。(I became used to listening to native speakers' English.)	12 (13)
6.	自分でもTED Talksを聞いて自主的な勉強をするようになった。(I came to listen to TED Talks on my own and study English voluntarily.)	8 (9)
7.	映像と字幕を使った教材なので、わからないことも推測でき自然と理解が高まった。(Because of the video and subtitles, I can guess the content by watching, so I was able to guess what I didn't understand.	6 (7)
8.	内容が面白いので教科書を使った勉強よりも興味が持てる。(Because the content is interesting, TED Talks are more enjoyable than textbooks.)	4 (4)

Note. N = 90.

However, as Table 7 shows, there were some negative responses. Some (22%, $n = 20$) mentioned that they wanted to study the talks more slowly and carefully because it was not easy for them to understand them. Another problem was that group/pair work did not go smoothly when their partners were not prepared. These pointed to the two changes that need to be made: more care should be given 1) to make the teaching materials easier to understand and 2) to create a classroom atmosphere where students can collaborate with each other by making sure they come to class prepared. Interestingly, some mentioned that they would rather study other topics than music. This needs to be considered, too, because teachers may assume that students want to study about content/topics related to their majors, but actually some may want to study about something which they are not familiar with in order to broaden their knowledge and perspectives.

Table 7

Students' Negative Responses

	Students' Negative Responses (English translation by the author)	n (%)
1.	もっとゆっくりと内容理解に時間をかけて、勉強したかった。(I wanted to study the talks more slowly.)	20 (22)
2.	英語のスピードが速く、内容が難しくて理解できないものがあった。(The speed of speaking was so fast that I couldn't understand some of the talks.	8 (9)
3.	プレゼンテーションに出てくる単語や文法も勉強したかった。(I wanted to study more vocabulary and grammar which appeared in the talks.)	4 (4)
4.	ペア・グループワークの相手によっては、授業の準備ができておらず、時間が無駄になることがあった。(Sometimes, my partner was not prepared for class and I felt like I was wasting time.)	4 (4)
5.	音楽以外の内容を学びたい。(I want to study talks about other topics, not music.)	4 (4)

| 6. | 日本語訳は最初に配らず、最後に配ってほしい。(I want the transcript distributed after we finish studying the talk.) | 3 (3) |

Note. *N* = 90.

11. Conclusion

The current paper described a content-based intervention designed to enhance motivation for learning English and music-related content. Both statistical and qualitative analyses of the results demonstrated that the intervention with the TED Talk was successful in getting music college students more motivated in learning not only English but also music-related content. Many students perceived the TED talks as useful and interesting materials to learn English and music-related content. One positive outcome of the intervention was that some students voluntarily watched TED Talks and studied English outside the classroom; that is, they became autonomous learners.

However, at the same time, it is important to note the negative comments given by some students who mentioned that the talks were difficult so they wanted to study them more slowly and carefully. Since authentic materials such as TED Talks can be overwhelming because they are intended for native speakers, it is necessary to make them more accessible by providing carefully structured scaffoldings. Although further research is required to assess the effectiveness of the intervention, content-based instruction seems to be an effective approach for fostering EFL learners' motivation if their interests, backgrounds, and individual needs are taken into consideration.

References

Bandura, A. (1986). From thought to action: Mechanisms of personal agency. *New Zealand Journal of Psychology, 15*, 1-17.

Brinton, D., Snow, M.A., & Wesche, M. B. (1989). *Content-based second language instruction.* Boston: Heinle & Heinle Publishers.

Csikszentmihalyi, Mihaly. (1990). Flow: The psychology of optimal experience. *Journal of Leisure Research, 24*(1), 93–94.

Clément, R. and Kruidenier, B. G. (1983), Orientations in second language acquisition: I. the effects of ethnic ty, milieu, and target language on their emergence. *Language Learning, 33* 273-291.

Curtain, H. A., & Pesola, C. A. (1994). Languages and children: Making the match (2nd ed.). NY: Longman.

Deci, E. L., & Ryan, R. M. (1985). *Intrinsic motivation and self-determination in human behaviour.* New York: Plenum Press.

Deci, E. L., & Ryan, R. M. (Eds.) (2002). *Handbook of self-determination research.* New York: University of Rochester Press.

Deci, E.L., Vallerand, R.J., Pelletier, L.G. and Ryan, R.M. (1991) Motivation and Education: The Self-Determination Perspective. *The Educational Psychologist, 26,* 325-346.

Dörnyei, Z. (2001). *Teaching and researching motivation.* Harlow: Longman.

Eccles, J. S. & Wigfield, A. (2002) Motivational beliefs, values, and goals. *Annual Review of Psychology, 53,* 109-132.

Gardner, R. C., & Lambert, R. C. (1959). Motivational variables in second language acquisition. *Canadian Journal of Psychology, 13,* 266-272.

Gardner, R. C., & Lambert, W. E. (1972). *Attitudes and motivation in second language learning.* Rowley, MA: Newbury.

Genesee, F. (1994). Integrating language and content: Lessons from immersion. Educational Practice Report 11. *National Center for Research on Cultural Diversity and Second Language Learning.*

Grabe, W., & Stoller, F.L. (1997). Content-based instruction: Research foundations. In Snow, M.A. & Brinton, D.M. (Eds.). *The content-based classroom: Perspectives on integrating language and content* (pp. 5-21). White Plains, NY: Longman.

Hiromori, T. (2006). The effects of educational intervention on L2 learners' motivational development. *JACET Bulletin, 43,* 1-14.

Lasagabaster, D. (2011). English achievement and student motivation in CLIL and

EFL settings. *Innovation in Language Learning and Teaching, 5,* 3-18.

Lukmani, M. Y. (1972). Motivation to Learn and language proficiency. *Language Learning, 22*(2), 261-273.

Met, M. (1991). *Content-based instruction: Defining terms, making decisions. NFLC Reports.* Washington, DC: The National Foreign Language Center.

Noels, K. A. (2001). Learning Spanish as a second language: Learners' orientations and perceptions of their teachers' communication style. *Language Learning, 51,* 107-144.

Noels, K. A., Pelletier, L., Clément, R., & Vallerand, R. (2003). Why are you learning a second language? Motivational orientations and self-determination theory. *Language Learning, 53,* 33-63.

Ruspini, E. 2002. *Introduction to longitudinal research.* London: Routledge.

Ryan, R. M. & Deci, E. L. (2000). Self-determination theory and the facilitation of intrinsic motivation, social development, and well-being. *American Psychologist, 55*(1), 68-78.

Schunk, D. H., Pintrich, P. R., & Meece, J., L. (2008). *Motivation in education (3rd ed.).* Upper Saddle River, NJ: Pearson Merrill Prentice Hall.

Takaesu, A. (2013). TED talks as an extensive listening resource for EAP students. In K. Kelly & J. Meddlecamp (Eds.) *Asian Focused ELT research and practice: Voices from the far edge* (pp. 108-120). Phnon Penh: IDP Education (Cambodia) Ltd.

Ushioda, E. (2011). Language learning motivation, self and identity: current theoretical perspectives. *Computer Assisted Language Learning, 24*(3), 199-210.

［本研究は、2016年大学英語教育学会第55回国際大会で発表しました。］

CHAPTER 3
Using Songs in EFL Classrooms
英語の歌を教材として使用した内容重視型授業

【概要】

　近年、日本における英語教育において急速に広まっている内容重視型教育（Content-based instruction; CBI）とは「教科学習」と「言語学習」を一つの授業内で統合したアプローチである。CBIは、教科内容を題材としてさまざまな活動を英語で行うことで、教科への理解を深めながら、英語の4技能及び発信力を高めることができる「統合的な指導法」として期待されている。本研究の目的は、CBIに基づいた英語授業実践を行い、その効果を検証することである。具体的には、「英語の歌」を教材として使用し、後半に英語の歌に関するプレゼンテーションを行った。学生が学期末に記入した振り返りを質的・量的に検証した結果、本実践は多くの学生のモチベーションを高め、英語を学ぶことへの意欲を高めたことが明らかになった。しかし、同時に、英語の歌詞の中には明示的でない文章や口語的な表現もあり、理解しにくいとの指摘もあったことから、英語の歌を教材として使うときの問題点も指摘する。

Keywords: Content-based instruction, music, songs, teaching English as a foreign language

1. Introduction

　During the last decade, there has been an increasing interest in an integrated instruction that combines content and language instruction including Content and Language Integrated Instruction (CLIL) or Content-Based Instruction (CBI). CBI is one of the widely practiced approaches to language teaching that focuses not only on the language itself but also on what is being taught through the language. One of the notable strengths of this approach is that it can make language learning more interesting, meaningful, and engaging by incorporating a specific type of content which learners are interested in into language classrooms. The current study reports on a CBI intervention that used music as the content of instruction in English classes for music college students.

2. Content-Based Language Instruction (CBI)

In a typical content-based classroom, a specific type of content is taught using a second/foreign language which students are learning. This approach views the target language as "the vehicle through which a specific type of content is learned" rather than as the immediate object of the study (Brinton, Snow, & Wesche, 1989, p.5). For example, in an EAP (English for academic purposes) context, students may study *Sociology* with materials written in English, using English as the tool of study and communication. As a result, students are able to develop both their knowledge of the content and linguistic ability in English.

One of the key issues of the CBI approach is the content, what to teach in the target language. There are differing views concerning what the content can be. For example, some researchers argue that the content should be related to curriculum concepts such as history, science, and math (e.g., Curtain and Pesola, 1994). Others suggest the content can be non-academic matters such as contemporary/social issues as long as it is interesting and important for the learner (e.g., Genesee, 1994). Met (1991) proposes that the content should be materials which are cognitively engaging and demanding for the learner. Despite these differences in the conception of the topics, perhaps, it is best to choose a subject or topic which is most suitable for learners, considering the curriculum of the context and students' academic interests and future needs.

Some of the strengths of CBI lie in the fact that it is an integrated approach for teaching second/foreign language. Brinton, Snow, & Wesche (1989) sums up the advantages of CBI as follows:

1. Students are able to think and learn a specific subject matter through the use of the target language.
2. CBI lends itself to the integration of the four traditional language skills.
3. CBI employs authentic materials which students have to interpret and evaluate.
4. CBI provides a forum where students can discuss materials.
5. Because CBI requires academic writing, students are able to synthesize facts and ideas from multiple sources.
6. CBI exposes students to a variety of language and study skills which prepare them for future academic tasks (Brinton, Snow, and Wesche, 1989, p. 2).

Furthermore, CBI can make language learning more interesting and motivating by allowing students to use the language to fulfill a real purpose of learning a specific type of knowledge. When students have high interest in the content being taught, it is highly likely for them to become more engaged in learning the content. For example, if music majors learn about music in their English class, it is likely that they become more motivated to learn the content and the language for two reasons. First, because they major in music, it is possible to assume that they enjoy studying about it. Second, because they already have prior knowledge about and experience in music, it is likely that they feel more competent or confident in learning the content and language. Grabe and Stoller (1997) argue that CBI classrooms generate increased motivation among students because "students are exposed to complex information and are involved in demanding activities which can lead to intrinsic motivation" (p. 20).

Despite these advantages, it is necessary to recognize some of the difficulties in practicing CBI in language classrooms. Because CBI is not explicitly focused on language learning, less proficient students may need more linguistic support such as grammar and vocabulary instruction. For example, CBI often uses authentic materials which tend to be challenging in terms of vocabulary, syntactic complexity, and lengthy sentences; therefore, explicit support should be provided in order to make the materials approachable and comprehensible. Furthermore, because it is not easy for such learners to communicate in the target language, it is necessary to give them linguistic support for output by providing a list of useful phrases for speaking and writing.

In summary, while content-based instruction can be challenging for less proficient L2/EFL learners, it is an effective and efficient method for language teaching because it merges language and content learning in one lesson. The merits of CBI include increased use of the target language, integration of the four language skills, and development of academic skills and content knowledge. Because of these strengths, it is expected that this type of instruction will be widely practiced in language classrooms in many countries including Japan.

3. The Study

The objective of the study was to investigate the effects of one type of content-based instruction (CBI) which used songs written in English as the content of instruction. The research question was posed as follows: "How do the participants of the study perceive the song-based intervention?". First, the outline of the intervention will be described including the participants, materials, and worksheets used to teach songs. Second, the students' perceptions of the intervention will be reported.

4. Method
4.1 Participants

The participants of the study were 163 music majors from eight intact English classes taught by the author. The students' majors included a variety of music majors: voice, piano, violin, wind instruments, percussion, music education, music therapy, and nursery education. All of them had been studying music and practicing one or more music instruments for several years before starting the college. Therefore, generally speaking, they had high interest in and enthusiasm for music. In terms of English proficiency, there was a wide range: some were intermediate, and others were basic (Eiken 3rd degree = 40 students, pre-2nd degree = 83, 2nd degree = 47).

4.2 Instrument of the Study

After the song intervention was conducted for 12 weeks, a 14-item questionnaire about the intervention was administered to explore how the CBI intervention was perceived by the students. Responses were collected using a Likert scale (1 = strongly disagree, 2 = disagree, 3 = agree, 4 = strongly disagree) and open-ended questions.

5. Content-Based Intervention

The 12-week intervention of the study consisted of two phases: studying English songs and giving a presentation about students' favorite songs. These two phases are described below.

5.1 Phase 1: Studying English Songs

During the first eight weeks, the students studied seven popular songs (Table 1). These songs were chosen considering the following criteria:

1. The song has a clear and meaningful message.
2. The song has timeless values.
3. Students can empathize with the message of the song.
4. Vocabulary and sentence structure are easy to understand.
5. The lyrics do not contain slang or ungrammatical expressions.
6. The singer's pronunciation is clear and easy to understand.
7. The melody of the song is beautiful and memorable.

Table 1
Songs Studied in Phase I (Week 2 – Week 9)

Title of the Song (Released Year)	Singer
Photograph (2014)	Ed Sheeran
Country Road (1971)	John Denver
Over the Rainbow (1939)	Judy Garland
Memory (1981)	Barbra Streisand
Puff, the Magic Dragon (1963)	Peter, Paul & Mary
You've got a Friend (1971)	Carol King
The Rose (1979)	Bette Midler

For each song, a worksheet was created with the following sections: 1) Background Questions, 2) Vocabulary, 3) Listening Exercise, 4) Pronunciation Practice, and 5) Summary & Reaction. A sample worksheet is shown below.

CHAPTER 3

[Sample Worksheet]
SONG 1: Over the Rainbow   Name _____

1. Background: Look up the answers to the questions using your PC or smartphone. (https://en.wikipedia.org/wiki/Over_the_Rainbow)	1. Why was this song written? 2. Who sang this song? 3. What is the genre of the song? 4. How popular was the song? 5. What do you think the song is about?
2. Vocabulary: Look up the words.	·lullaby ·behind ·melt
3. Lyrics: Listen to the song and write down missing words. https://www.youtube.com/watch?v=1HRa4X07jd	Somewhere over the _____ way up high There's a _____ that I heard of once in a _____ Somewhere over the rainbow skies are _____ And the dreams that you dare to dream really do come true_____ Someday I'll wish upon a _____ And wake up where the _____ are far Behind me Where troubles melt like lemon _____ way above the chimney _____ That's where you'll _____ me
4. Pronunciation: Listen to the song and mark linking and stress.	1. Underline the words which are linked 2. Circle the words stressed. 3. Read the lyrics aloud.
5. What is the song about? Discuss the meaning of the song with your partner and write your ideas.	
6. What is your reaction to the song?	

These songs were taught following the procedures described in Table 2.

Table 2
Song Teaching Procedures

Timeline	Assignment/Classroom Activities
1st week	Assign homework: 1. answer background Qs, 2. listen to the song, 3. look up vocabulary, 4. use the Internet to answer Qs.
2nd week	Classroom activity: 1. check homework answers, 2. listen to the song, 3. pair work to understand the content and discuss meanings/messages of the song, 3. assign homework (writing a summary of and a reaction to the song).
3rd week	Classroom activity: 1. Check homework answers (exchanging summaries and reactions in groups), 2. share ideas and evaluate the song.

5.2 Phase 2: "My Favorite Song" Presentation

In the second phase (Week 10 - Week 13) of the semester, the students prepared individual presentations about their favorite songs and presented them as the final project of the class. Instructions on how to prepare the presentation were given (Table 3). Furthermore, to ensure successful performance, lectures were given on effective presentation skills as well as some of the useful presentation phrases.

Table 3
Instruction for the Song Presentation

How to prepare your presentation
1. Give a presentation about your favorite English song.
2. Choose a song whose lyrics are meaningful and easy to understand.
3. Make Google slides (5~6 slides) which include the following sections:
1) Title and singer
2) Why you chose the song
3) Background of the singer (group/singer) and the song
4) Lyrics and vocabulary, and YouTube address

5) the message of the song and your reaction to the song
6) Final words
3. Give a 3~5-minute presentation using the slides. Play part of the song using YouTube.
4. After you finish your presentation, ask classmates for questions and comments.

The students chose a wide variety of songs for their presentations, including famous folk songs, recent pop/rock music, or old jazz numbers. Table 4 shows some of them.

Table 4
Songs Chosen by the Students

Song Titles and Singers
Bridge over the troubled water by Simon & Garfunkel
Just the way you are by Bruno Mars
Moon River by Andy Williams
You raise me up by Celtic Woman
Singing in the rain by Gene Kelly
Penny lane by the Beatles
This is me by Keela Settle
Scarborough fair by Simon & Garfunkel
A whole new world by Brad Kane and Lea Salonga
Beauty and the beast by Peabo Bryson
Thousand miles by Vanessa Carlton
Born this way by Lady Gaga

Overall, the students gave successful and interesting presentations, using slides with detailed information about the song and colorful pictures and illustrations. Even though many of them were not used to giving a presentation in English, this presentation appeared to be not so challenging because its theme was related to music and the structure of the presentation was explicitly instructed. Furthermore, it appeared that they enjoyed listening to each other's presentations with songs.

6. Students' Perceptions of the Content-Based Instruction with Songs

At the end of the semester, students' perceptions of the CBI intervention with songs were collected and analyzed using both quantitative and qualitative analyses. Table 5 shows their responses to 14 Likert-scale questions.

Table 5

Students' Perceptions of the Song Intervention

Questionnaire Items	(English translation by the author)	M	SD
1 クラスメートの英語の歌のプレゼンは楽しかった。	I enjoyed my classmates' presentations.	3.62	0.53
2 英語の歌を勉強するのは楽しかった。	It was fun to study English songs.	3.56	0.55
3 英語の歌を勉強することにより、英語学習への興味が高まった。	I became more interested in studying English by studying English songs.	3.44	0.62
4 英語でコミュニケーションを取るのは楽しかった。	It was fun to communicate in English	3.34	0.65
5 英語の歌のプレゼン準備と発表は楽しかった。	I enjoyed preparing and giving the presentation.	3.33	0.73
6 クラスメートと様々な話題を英語で話すことができた。	I was able to talk about a variety of topics with my classmates in English.	3.21	0.69
7 授業中は英語を話した。	I spoke English during the class.	3.16	0.58
8 英語学習へのモチベーションが高まった。	I became more interested in studying English.	3.14	0.73
9 プレゼンは自分が思っていることを英語で表現できた。	I was able to express what I wanted to say in English.	3.01	0.72
10 今学期は英語の勉強を頑張った。	I studied English hard	2.99	0.63

	this semester.		
11 英語の発音が良くなった。	My English pronunciation improved.	2.89	0.80
12 英語力が上がったと思う。	My English improved.	2.87	0.72
13 授業外でも英語を自ら進んで定期的に勉強した。	I studied English outside the classroom, too.	2.59	0.80
14 自分の英語力に自信が持てた。	I feel more confident about my English ability.	2.55	0.73

Note. Responses were collected using the following Likert scales: 1 そう思わない、2 あまりそう思わない、3 そう思う、4 大変そう思う

The descriptive statistics of the questionnaire data indicated that the students perceived the first phase of the CBI intervention overwhelmingly positive and enjoyable. Most of them stated that they enjoyed learning English through songs (M = 3.56) and became more motivated to study English (M = 3.44). The second phase of the intervention with song presentations was equally favorably perceived: students responded that they not only enjoyed their classmates' presentations (M = 3.62) but also presenting about their favorite songs (M = 3.33). Thus, the results of the Likert scale questionnaire demonstrated that the intervention was positively perceived by the students.

Responses to open-ended questions are shown in Table 6. As the quantitative results above indicated, many of them mentioned that it was effective to learn English through songs.

Table 6

Students' Open-ended Responses (Positive)

Responses (in original words)	(English translation by the author)
1 初めて毎回の課題が苦にならないと思った。	For the first time, I didn't mind doing English homework.
2 今まで英語の授業はつまらないと思っていたが、文章でも音楽が関わってくると楽しいと思えた。	I used to think English classes were boring, but now I enjoy studying English through music.
3 文法で英語を学ぶよりも、歌だと自然に耳に残って覚えるし、メロディーの感じから悲しい気持ちなのか、うれしいのか、心情や背景が頭に入ってくるのでわかりやすい。	When I study English with music, I can remember English phrases naturally, and also the melody helps me understand the feeling and background of the song.
4 内容が良い詩が多くて、ただ教科書を見て読むよりも身につく。	Because the songs include memorable lyrics, I can learn them well, rather than just studying textbooks.

Interestingly, one student mentioned that she enjoyed doing homework for the first time because it was about music. Several students mentioned that they remembered English phrases more than the time when they studied ordinary textbooks because these phrases were accompanied by beautiful melodies.

However, at the same time, some students pointed out some problems in using songs as the learning materials (Table 7). For example, some lyrics are difficult to understand because they do not include detailed information about the context of the song or they omit specific references to pronouns. Or sometimes it is hard to understand what is spoken because of the melody and rhythm. These responses pointed out importance considerations for teachers when they choose songs as teaching materials. That is, careful attention should be paid to lyrics and melodies in choosing songs for teaching.

Table 7
Students' Open-ended Responses (Negative)

Responses (in original words)	Translation by the author
1 歌だとリズムに歌詞が入っていくので聞き取ることに苦戦する。	Listening to songs can be more difficult because of the rhythm.
2 英語の歌詞を日本語にするのが普通の文章以上に難しい	It is difficult to translate lyrics into Japanese.
3 歌になるとメロディが下がる音だったりするので、実際に話すイントネーションと少し違う。	Songs may carry different intonation patterns from ordinary speaking.
4 英語の歌から文法を学ぶのは難しい	It is difficult to study grammar using songs.

7. Conclusion

The content-based intervention with songs seems to have successfully enhanced college students' motivation for learning English. Most of the students reported that it was meaningful and enjoyable to study English with songs. It was notable that some reported that they were able to transform their negative views of learning English due to the song intervention. However, some students reported some of the problematic aspects including the difficulties of understanding lyrics, grammar, and pronunciation. Despite these limitations, the authors argue that songs are useful and effective materials for learning and teaching a second/foreign language.

References

Brinton, D., Snow, M.A., & Wesche, M. B. (1989). *Content-based second language instruction.* Boston: Heinle & Heinle Publishers.

Curtain, H. A., & Pesola, C. A. (1994). Languages and children: Making the match (2nd ed.). NY: Longman.

Genesee, F. (1994). *Integrating language and content: Lessons from immersion.*

  Educational Practice Report.
Grabe, W., & Stoller, F.L. (1997). Content-based instruction: Research foundations. In Snow, M.A. & Brinton, D.M. (Eds.). *The content-based classroom: Perspectives on integrating language and content* (pp. 5-21). White Plains, NY: Longman.
Met, M. (1991). Learning language through content: Learning content through language. *Foreign Language Annals, 24*.

［本論文は国立音楽大学研究紀要 52 巻（2018）に発表した論文に加筆したものです。］

CHAPTER 4
Using Children's Literature in EFL Classrooms
絵本・児童文学を使用した英語授業

【概要】

　絵本に代表される児童文学は、大人のための第 2 言語（L2）・外国語学習教材として利用されることは少なく、大人にはふさわしくないジャンルであるという意見はいまだに根強い。しかし、近年、「言語を学ぶための教材」としての絵本の効果が認められ、アジア諸国をはじめとする世界の様々な国で、絵本を大人の言語学習に活用した実践・研究報告が増えてきた。本論文の第1の目的は、先行研究を参照しながら、絵本がなぜ大人のための言語学習教材として効果的であるかを述べることにある。具体的には、絵本の「普遍的なテーマ性」、「ビジュアルな絵やイラストによる言語理解を促進する効果」、「読むことへの興味・関心を高める情意的効果」、「文法や語彙教材としての価値」などを指摘する。第2の目的は、著者が行った「絵本を使った英語授業実践」について報告し、大学生を対象に行った絵本を教材として使用した実践が、彼らのモチベーションにどのような影響をもたらしたかを報告することである。この授業で使用された絵本、リーディング・アクテビティ、学生の感想なども紹介する。

Keywords: children's literature, picture books, adult L2 learners, L2 reading

1. Introduction

　　Children's literature can be a powerful tool in teaching second language (L2)/foreign language (FL) reading. It is one genre of authentic literature, which addresses important and familiar issues in ordinary people's lives. Picture books, in particular, are suited for language learners because such books are often filled with vivid and colorful illustrations which help them understand the plot or the story, regardless of linguistic and cultural barriers. Despite these merits, it appears that many L2 educators and practitioners are still hesitant in using children's literature with adults because they might regard it as too childish to read. The present paper argues that children's literature, in fact, represents an invaluable source of authentic literature to be used in the L2 college classroom if appropriate books/stories are chosen and taught with suitable teaching methodology for mature learners.

This paper consists of four sections. First, general features and values of picture books are explained Second, specific values of such literature in language learning contexts are described. Third, several criteria for choosing appropriate books for adult language learners are listed. Finally, a study which utilized picture books written in English as the reading materials will be reported to explore how such literature can be successfully utilized in language learning classrooms for adults.

2. Children's Literature in Adult Education

In recent years, there has been a growing interest in using children's literature in the education of young adult and adult learners. Those who support this trend claim that children's literature is highly appropriate for developing older learners' literary competence, interest in reading, critical thinking skills, spiritual growth, and intercultural awareness (English, 2000; Bland, 2009). According to English (2000), children's books are "immensely suitable" in adult education because such books are written by "adults who are often resolving adult dilemmas when writing, and more specifically, they are seeking to understand and explain their relationships and interpersonal issues when they write" (p. 14).

A notable Japanese writer, Kunio Yanagida (2006) has repeatedly pointed out that picture books are written not only for children but also for adults of all ages because they are filled with insightful reflections about life and how to live, resonating with the lives of grown-ups:

> Picture books represent one type of a literary genre which is written for children, but it can be appreciated by people of all ages beyond generation and age differences. Picture books are different from religious sermons or moral education in that they make us think about essential aspects of human lives, including humor, wisdom, grief, separation, thoughtfulness, compassion, encouragement, love, spirituality, and life itself. Picture books create a three-dimensional world by compactly merging carefully-worded sentences and the effects of actual voices produced by reading aloud. Reading picture books slowly and repeatedly brings out deep compassion and awareness in readers' hearts as if water colors slowly and steadily spread over paper (p. 15). (This passage was translated by the author from Japanese to English.)

As stated above, children's books are often based on the author's personal memories and reflections about their own personal lives and experiences; therefore, such books can be appropriate for older readers who may have had similar experiences.

Erika (Heidenreich, 2007), one of the books recommended by Yanagida, for example, can be deeply appreciated by older learners who understand the strong bond and love between parents and their children. This story is about a Jewish woman (named Erika) who survived the Holocaust. In the opening scene of the story, Erika and her parents were about to be sent to a concentration camp by the Nazis. Erika, who then was a baby, was held by her mother. Suddenly the mother threw Erika to a complete stranger who was watching them being taken away to the camp. This scene is quite shocking for readers, but then soon they realize that the mother did this to save Erika's life, hanging onto a slim chance of her survival. Adult readers can understand the painful and sad feelings of the mother, remembering the historical background of the story and imagining what it was like to live in such a dark period.

Another book suitable for adults is a bestselling picture book, *Love you Forever* (Munsch, 1986). This story is about a middle-aged man who looks back on his relationship with his mother, starting from his baby age. It portrays how their relationship evolved as both of them grew older. The last scene, in which he holds up his mother who has weakened due to her old age, is particularly moving for adult readers because they can imagine the warm bond between the mother and the son and predict that the mother will not live long. Even though this story is categorized as a picture book for children, it is easy to speculate that children will not be able to understand the full implications of the content until they grow much older and have similar experiences. The book deeply moves the heart of adults who have gone through such major life events as teenage rebellion, graduation, marriage, parenting, aging, and separation. There are many other books which deal with similar themes, such as *The Giving Tree* (Silverstein, 1998), *Someday* (McGhee, 2007), and *Badger's Parting Gifts* (Varley, 2002). English (2000) sums up the value of children's literature in adult education: children's literature is especially suited for adults "because of its length, clarity, and direct focus on a theme" (p. 17).

3. Special Features of Children's Books for Adult Language Learners

There are a number of features of children's literature that make it useful for language learners including adults and college students (Ho, 2000; Hsiu-Chih, 2008; Smallwood, 1991, 1992, 1998; Zhang, 2008).

Smallwood (1998) points out: "Because high quality children's literature is characterized by economy of words, stunning illustrations, captivating but quickly moving plots, and universal themes, carefully chosen books can offer educational benefits for adult English language learners as well as for children" (p. 1). Hashim (1999) aptly summarizes why such books are suitable for L2 readers:

> The student could read these short books quickly, gaining confidence that comes with accomplishment. In addition, the language of the text builds on and repeats phrases, thus facilitating the learner's interaction with it. This repetitiveness helps the learner to grasp important points and to provide an adequate synopsis of what is being read.... Because there is not much to remember, with guidance the learner can recall significant events in the stories for retelling. There is also less need for the learner to interpret the story since the storylines are simple. This reduces the fear of not being able to understand the content, which might affect learner confidence. In general, the feelings of success and achievement that come with being able to read these texts and understand stories written in English can motivate learners to read more, improve their reading and understanding (p. 4).

Picture books, therefore, are comprehensible, easy to remember, and effective for building confidence in reading. Because readers can experience success in reading, this leads to the feeling of competence, which then fosters motivation for further reading.

In summary, the values of children's books for adults can be classified into the following eight categories.

1) Confidence building: Children's books builds confidence in reading because they often include simpler language, shorter stories, less abstract ideas, and less complicated themes (Hai-yan, 2008).
2) Interesting stories: plots are interesting and captivating, so students can be interested in the story and go on reading without being aware of it (Hsiu-Chih, 2008). Ho (2000) points out that children's literature can stimulate personal involvement, arouse readers' interest, and provoke strong positive reactions from them (p. 260).
3) Linguistic value: Children's books are written using natural and comprehensible language so they expose L2 learners to authentic reading materials which otherwise might not be accessible. Also, children's literature promotes overall language proficiency (Smallwood, 1992). Because sentences are shorter and similar expressions and phrases are repeated, it is easy to learn sentence structures. Vocabulary is introduced in context with the help of pictures, so it is easy to guess meanings of new words and remember them (Bland, 2009).
4) Focus on meaning: Readers can focus on meaning rather than mechanical aspects of language. Hsiu-Chih (2008) indicates that "[children's] literature allows readers to shift from mechanical language learning to a more personal meaningful context" (p. 50).
5) Artistic/Visual value: Pictures can serve to clarify the text and facilitate language learning (Hsiu-Chih, 2008). According to Smallwood (1992), good pictures are similar to universal language which can be understood without language barriers. Pictures help even less proficient learners understand stories and enhance their self-efficacy in reading.
6) Social value: Children's literature often deals with personal and

social issues which can be found in ordinary people's lives, for instance, developing close ties with family and friends or learning the importance of sharing and cooperating with others (Hai-yan, 2008). As a result, it heightens students' awareness of social, moral, and ethical issues.

7) Familiar issues: Topics are generally more familiar to students than those of academic texts. So students can easily voice their opinions, talk about their own experiences, and share them with their classmates. This often leads to the creation of a "reading community" where students can learn from each other.

8) Cultural value: Children's literature provides rich cultural information which facilitates intercultural awareness and understanding (Ho, 2000). Especially, those who have never been to other countries can indirectly experience what is like to grow up in such countries by reading picture books. With the help of colorful and artistic illustrations, they can easily identify many similarities and differences with their own cultures and deepen understanding of the people in these countries.

4. Criteria for Book Selection

Because some children's books are obviously intended only for small children, it is true that not all such books are suitable for mature readers. Therefore, it is necessary to choose quality literature which is well-suited for mature readers. Hai-yan (2008), for instance, recommends stories which transcend cultural boundaries and appeal to people of different backgrounds. Furthermore, it is important to look for books which have original, appealing ideas that may stimulate mature learners' curiosity and interest. In ESL contexts, Smallwood (1992) has suggested the following six criteria for choosing books for adult learners (p. 1):

(a) Does it relate to your curriculum objectives?
(b) Does it include adults?
(c) Are there clear illustrations that help tell the story?
(d) Does it contain repeated, predictable language patterns?
(e) Does it use language only slightly beyond the level of the learners?
(f) Is there a cultural or multicultural perspective?

These criteria are useful when language teachers choose books for their students. In summary, it is necessary to consider adult learners' interests and backgrounds as well as classroom objectives and language goals in order to select suitable books for them.

5. Teaching Children's Literature in the L2 College Classroom

In order to demonstrate how picture books can be utilized in language learning contexts, this section reports the author's teaching practice with college students in Japan. The following sections describe the teaching context, the participants, the reading processes, the picture books read, and students' perceptions of the use of picture books.

5.1 Context of Teaching

Picture books were used in two English classes (*English for Communication*) at a music college in Tokyo. The students were music majors, including piano, computer music, composition, music education, and wind instruments. Their English proficiency was from basic to intermediate (approximately from Eiken pre-2nd degree to pre-1st degree). There were three returnees who had spent more than one year in English speaking countries. The number of the students in the two classes was 20 respectively. Each class met twice a week for a 90-minute lesson. Generally, the students were motivated to study English, and they usually completed assignments. The atmosphere in the classroom was friendly and cooperative, and most of them punctually attended classes. The classroom language was basically English, and the students usually spoke English with each other during classroom activities. Picture books were used as supplementary reading materials.

5.2 Teaching Procedures

Picture books were taught in four different phases: before reading, during reading, after reading, and repeated reading. In each process, students conducted different reading activities while practicing a variety of reading strategies. The activities and reading strategies used during these four phases are listed below (Table 1).

Table 1
Process of Using Picture Books

	Process	Activity	Reading Strategies Practiced
1.	Before reading	Look at the book cover and title. Talk about them.	Activating background knowledge. Predicting the content.
2.	During reading	Listen to the story. Ask questions and make comments.	Understanding main ideas. Guessing the meanings of unknown words.
3.	After reading	Recall the content by asking and answering questions. Discuss main ideas and exchange reactions to the story. Learn the linguistic features in the story.	Summarizing the story. Analyzing the theme of the story. Reacting to the story.

| 4. Repeated reading | Practice reading (with Teacher or CD). Reading aloud. | Critically evaluating the story. |

5.3 Book Selection Criteria

Following the guidelines suggested by Smallwood (1992) as well as students' interests, the following were considered when choosing appropriate books for the students.

Table 2

Criteria for Book Selection

Features of Books	Criteria
Length of the story	300 words ~ 1000 words
Vocabulary Difficulty	Two ~ three new words per page
Structure	Easy to understand without translating into Japanese (e.g., repeated phrases, shorter sentences, simple sentence structure)
Plot	Stimulating and engaging narratives possibly with surprise or humor
Theme	Common themes often found in ordinary people's lives (e.g., aging, growing-up, family)
Protagonists	Not only children but also adults appear as chief characters
Illustrations	Attractive, explicit pictures with beautiful colors

5.4 Picture Books, Synopses, Students' Reactions

In total, five books were used as reading materials. Table 3 shows the books, including the title, synopses, excerpts, as well as students' reactions to them.

Table 3

Book Titles, Synopses, and Students' Reactions

Title of the book (Author, Year)	Synopsis	Students' Reactions to the book
Puff, the Magic Dragon (Yarrow, 2008)	This story was originally written as a song. The author wrote the picture book version in 2008. Puff, a magic dragon, has a good friend, Jack. Although they enjoy spending time together, when Jack grows up, he stops coming to see Puff. Puff becomes lonely and sad, but one day a surprise happens.	"I love the song, but I didn't know there was a story. I was impressed with the beautiful picture and the change the author made in the story version of the song." "I was able to understand how sad Puff was when he lost his friend." "It is a story which I want to read with my children."
Owl at Home (Lobel, 1982)	Short hilarious and delightful tales about Owl's cute misunderstandings and mistakes.	"This story is so funny. I love the cute owl's desperate efforts to deal with his dilemmas." "Although I know Owl is stupid, I cannot help loving him for his humor and seriousness.
Kissing Hand (Penn, 1993)	A story about a raccoon child, Chester, who is about to start school. He is worried about going to Owl's school, leaving his mother at home. His mother encourages him to go to school by teaching him a special magic.	"I remembered the time when I started school. Like Chester, it was a difficult moment and my mother helped me." "Reading the story, I realized how lonely my mother felt when I started school." "My heart became warm. I think mother's love is strong and it makes children strong. When I was an elementary school pupil, I didn't want to go to school, but my mother didn't scold me and watched over me."

Miss Rumphius (Cooney, 1982)	A woman's biography narrated by her grandchild. All her life Alice thought about how she could make the world more beautiful. After traveling all over the world for many years, she finally settles down in a beautiful village near the sea. In the village, she makes her dream come true by planting beautiful flowers called Lupine everywhere in the village.	"I was touched by the message --I want to make the world more beautiful." "Like Alice, I want to make the world more beautiful by playing beautiful music." "This story moved me because a woman kept pursuing her dream and finally it came true." "I would like to travel around the world like Alice." "This book gave me a chance to think about what I would like to accomplish in my life."
The Old Woman Who Named Things (Lyrant, 2000)	A story about an old woman who lives alone, surrounded by her favorite furniture and car. She has given a name to each of them. Because she has outlived her family and friends, she is afraid of losing another close one so she avoids personal contact. One day, however, she meets a dog. First, she is afraid of getting close to him, but gradually her life begins to change because of the dog.	"The loneliness of the old woman touched my heart. It must be hard to lose family and friends. I was happy when she finally met the dog and gave him a name." "At first, I didn't understand why the woman gave names to things, but as I read the story, I was able to sympathize with her and understand the lonely situation she was in."

Note. The students' reactions were translated into English by the author.

5.5 Students' Perceptions of Reading Picture Books

At the end of the semester, a questionnaire was conducted to investigate how the students perceived the use of picture books in college English classes. Three questions were asked: 1) "How did you perceive the use of picture books in the class?"; 2) "What are the effects of picture books in learning English?"; and 3) "What do you think of adults' reading picture books?. Generally, most of the students responded to the first question overwhelmingly positively. They stated that reading picture books was so enjoyable that it was not like "studying". They described picture books as stimulating, healing, heart-warming, refreshing, and adorable. Some mentioned that reading picture books was so engaging that they felt more motivated to read English.

As for the second question on the effects of studying English through picture books, the students mentioned that 1) they were able to learn useful expressions and vocabulary because they appeared in the stories repeatedly; 2) they were able to guess the meanings of unknown words because of pictures and illustrations; 3) they were able to understand English without translating sentences into Japanese; and 4) reading the stories aloud helped them understand the story. Therefore, students reported that picture books helped them learn English.

Concerning the third question, all of the students responded that adults should read picture books. Some of the major reasons they listed are: 1) adults may be able to interpret picture books in different ways from those of children; 2) they can remember how they used to feel in their childhood; 3) they can become more flexible and gain new perspectives in their minds; and 4) picture books are written not only for children but also for adults. One student indicated that she used to think that picture books were too childish for adults, but she changed her mind after reading the picture books in the class. She mentioned that adults should read such literature because it refreshes adults' minds. Thus, the students' responses generally indicated that they favored reading picture books in English classrooms. Furthermore, they reported that it is effective to learn English through picture books.

6. Conclusion

Although children's literature has long been considered to be intended only for children, this paper has argued that the literature can be one of the most effective teaching materials available for older and mature language learners. Especially, picture books are valuable materials because words and art in them create meaning greater than either one alone.

The first part of this paper presented the merits of picture books, including affective and linguistic values. However, in order to utilize them effectively, it is essential to select books wisely, considering the theme and language of the books. The second part of the paper described how picture books were used in the author's college English class. The students' positive reactions to the books read in the class demonstrated that they found the picture books to be stimulating and valuable reading materials. Furthermore, the experience of reading the picture books fostered positive attitudes toward reading. Although the effects of picture books in language classrooms require further empirical investigation, it is hoped that children's literature will be more widely used in language classrooms.

References

Bland, J. (2009). *Children's literature and learner empowerment*. New York: Continuum International Publishing Group Ltd.
Cooney, B. (1982). Miss Rumphius. New York: Penguin Press.
English, L. M. (2000). Children's literature for adults: a meaningful paradox. *PAACE Journal of Lifelong Learning, 9*, 13-23.
Heidenreich, E. (2007). *Erika*. New York: Kein + Aber /Audios
Hashim, F. (1999). Enabling a reader through picture books: a case study. *Literacy Across Cultures, 3*(1). From http://www2.aasa.ac.jp/~dcdycus/LAC99/MAR99/ CMAR99.HTM
Ho, L. (2000). Children's literature in adult education. *Children's Literature in*

Education, 31(4), 259-270.

Hsiu-Chih, S. (2008). The value of English picture story books. *ELT Journal, 62*(1), 47-54.

Lobel, A. (1982). *Owl at home.* New York: HarperCollins.

Lyrant, C. (2000). *The old woman who named things.* Singapore: Voyager Books.

McGhee, A. (2007). *Someday.* New York: Simon and Schuster.

Penn, A. (1993). *Kissing hand.* Hong Kong: Regent Publishing Press.

Munsch, R. M. (1986). *Love you forever.* New York: Firefly.

Silverstein, S. (1998). *The giving tree.* New York: Harper Collins.

Smallwood, B. A. (1991). *The literature connection: A read-aloud guide for multicultural classrooms.* Reading, MA: Addison Wesley.

Smallwood, B. A. (1992). *Children's literature for adult ESL literacy.* Washington, DC. National Clearinghouse on Literacy Education. (ERIC Document Reproduction Service No. ED 353 864).

Smallwood, B. (1998) *Using Multicultural Children's Literature in Adult ESL Classes.* National Clearinghouse for ESL Literacy Education Washington DC ERIC. Retrieved from http://www.ericdigests.org/1999-4/using.htm

Varley, S. (2002). *Badger's parting gifts.* New York: Harper Collins.

Yanagida, K. (2006). *Otonaga ehonni namidasuru-toki.* Heibonsha: Tokyo.

Yarrow, P. (2008). *Puff the magic dragon.* New York: Macmillan.

Zhang, Hai-yan. (2008). Values and limitations of children's literature in adult language education. *US-China Foreign Language, 6*(3), 18-21.

[本論文は国立音楽大学研究紀要47巻（2013）に発表した論文に加筆したものです。]

CHAPTER 5
"Choice" in EFL Classrooms
英語の授業における「チョイス」

【概要】

　本研究の目的は、英語の授業に、学習者が自ら選ぶ機会、つまり「チョイス」を取り入れることが、どのように彼らのモチベーションに影響を与えるかを調査することである。東京にある音楽大学で行われた必修英語授業において、70名の音楽専攻の学生を対象に、"Talk like a TED speaker"(「TEDスピーカーのように話してみよう」)というプレゼンテーション・プロジェクトを行った。このプロジェクトは、2つの局面から成り立っており、まず、学生はいくつかのTED Talksの学習を通して、英語とプレゼンテーション・スキルを学び、次に自分の選んだトピックについてプレゼンテーションを行った。その後、学生が自らトピックを選んだことをどのように感じたかについて、アンケート調査を行った。その結果、41名(59%)の学生はトピックを自分で選んだことで、モチベーションが高まったと答えた。一方、自分で選ぶよりも、教員からトピックを与えられるほうが良いと答えた学生は19名(24%)であった。興味深いことに、プレゼンテーション終了後に、「トピックを教師から与えられるよりも自ら選んだほうが良い」と考えを変えた学生も9名(13%)いた。その理由としては、「プレゼンテーションから多くを学んだことから、自分で選んだほうが良いと思った」と記述していた。これらの結果から、多くの学生は自分で選ぶことを好む傾向にあるが、そうではない学生も少なからずいること、また自分でトピックを選び、やりがいのある経験をすることで、自ら選ぶことを肯定的に思い始める学生もいることが明らかになった。

Keywords: motivation, autonomy, choice, Western/Eastern cultures

1. Introduction

The purpose of the current study is to explore EFL learners' perceptions of "choice" in Japan. According to self-determination theory, giving choice in educational contexts increases autonomy, and the increased autonomy results in higher intrinsic motivation for learning (Deci & Ryan, 1985). Some cross-cultural researchers, however, have argued that this assumption does not hold true in Eastern cultures where people do not value "autonomy" as much as those in Western cultures do (Markus & Kitayama, 2003). To shed light on this controversy about the role of choice in Eastern cultures, the current study explores how college students in Japan perceive choice provided in classrooms.

2. Literature Review

The present study is guided by self-determination theory (SDT) (Deci & Ryan, 1985), a theory of motivation which has been applied to numerous studies on second language learning and teaching as one of the reliable frameworks for language learners' motivation (Noels, Pelletier, Clément & Vallerand, 2000). In this literature review section, SDT is briefly reviewed, and then some studies on cross-cultural views of "choice" are introduced.

2.1 Self-Determination Theory

Self-determination theory (SDT) is "an empirically based theory of human motivation, development, and wellness" (Deci & Ryan, 2008, p. 182). This theory addresses social-contextual conditions that promote versus prevent the natural processes of self-motivation and healthy psychological development (Deci & Ryan, 1985; Deci & Ryan, 2000). One of the central features of SDT is the distinction between two types of human behaviors: intrinsically motivated behaviors and extrinsically motivated ones. The former is performed out of interest and curiosity while the latter originates from outside of one's self due to external pressure or control.

This distinction can be explained using the notion of "the locus of causality." When individuals take action based on their internal drive or force, the locus of causality is within themselves; therefore, the regulatory process involves their own volition or "choice." However, when they take action because they are "externally propelled into action" (Ryan & Deci, 2000, p. 55), the locus of causality lies outside of their selves. Therefore, the regulatory process involves "compliance" (Deci, Vallerand, Pelletier, & Ryan, 1991, p. 327). Basic tenets of these two motivations are briefly explained below.

Intrinsic motivation is defined as "the doing of an activity for its inherent satisfactions rather than for some separable consequence" (Ryan & Deci, 2000, p. 56). When intrinsically motivated, individuals are spontaneously moved to act for the enjoyment or challenge that accompanies the given task. For example, when people are absorbed in playing soccer just for the fun of it, they are intrinsically motivated because they engage in the sport following their inner desire to do so. Alternatively, when people are engrossed in reading a mystery and cannot stop reading, they are driven by their intrinsic interest in the story itself.

Extrinsic motivation, on the other hand, refers to behaviors that are considered a means to an end (Deci & Ryan, 1985). In other words, extrinsically motivated behaviors are instrumental because they are performed not out of strong interest in the activity itself, but to achieve some separable outcomes. For instance, if college students enrolled in a history class submit an assignment only to pass the class, their actions are extrinsically motivated because the action is taken to attain the separable outcome of satisfying the class requirements.

The focus on intrinsic motivation within SDT is explained by a sub-theory known as cognitive evaluation theory (CET) (Deci & Ryan, 1985;

Ryan & Deci, 2000). CET suggests that social environments can facilitate or forestall intrinsic motivation by supporting versus blocking people's fulfillment of their psychological needs. Based on the findings of empirical research, CET is focused primarily on three psychological needs, "competence, autonomy, and relatedness, which, when satisfied, yield enhanced self-motivation and mental health and, when prevented, lead to decreased motivation and self-being" (Ryan & Deci, 2000, p. 68). Competence is defined as one's perceived abilities in performing given tasks and "being efficacious in performing the requisite actions." Relatedness is defined as "developing secure and satisfying connections with others in one's social environment." Autonomy is defined as "being self-initiating and self-regulating of one's own actions" (Deci, Vallerland, Pelletier, and Ryan, 1991, p. 327). CET posits that these three factors are essential for positive behaviors and the enhancement of intrinsic motivation, which result in high-quality learning and creativity (Ryan & Deci, 2000).

In summary, self-determination theory makes a critical distinction between intrinsic and extrinsic behaviors: autonomous behaviors that emanate from one's sense of self and externally controlled behaviors performed because of outside pressure or control. This theory postulates that promoting greater self-determination is an important developmental goal. Furthermore, it posits that support for learners' feeling of competence, autonomy, and relatedness is essential for human development (Ryan & Deci, 2000).

2.2 Autonomy Support in Classrooms

In fostering motivation for learning, teachers' autonomy support plays an important role in classrooms (Deci & Ryan, 1985). Autonomy support implies promoting choice, minimizing pressure to perform tasks in a certain way, and encouraging initiative (Deci & Ryan, 2000). Teachers need to provide autonomy support by identifying, nurturing, and building students' inner motivational resources (Deci & Ryan, 1985). According to Niemiec and Ryan (2009), "Students' autonomy can be supported by teachers' minimizing the salience of evaluating pressure and any sense of coercion in the classroom, as well as by maximizing students' perceptions of having a voice and choice in those academic activities in which they are engaged" (p. 139). Specifically, Deci et al. (1994) suggested that educators should provide the following five conditions in classrooms: 1) providing a meaningful rationale, 2) acknowledging negative feelings, 3) using noncontrolling language, 4) offering meaningful choices, and 5) nurturing inner motivational choices.

2.3 Choice and Intrinsic Motivation

Many scholars have suggested that offering meaningful choice increases levels of intrinsic motivation and enhances performance on a variety of tasks (Deci & Ryan, 1985; Flowerday & Schraw, 2000; Rotter, 1966; Taylor, 1989). The link between the provision of choice and intrinsic motivation has been researched by some psychologists (Deci, 1975; Deci & Ryan, 1985). In one study, participants worked on puzzles under two conditions: one was choosing the puzzles themselves, and another was having the experimenter choose the puzzles. The findings of the study demonstrated that the participants worked on more puzzles when they chose the puzzles themselves (Zuckerman et al., 1978).

Another study found that even a minor choice not directly related to the activity itself can increase intrinsic motivation (Cordova & Lepper, 1996). In this study, participants worked on a computer math game. When they were able to select their own usernames during the game, their intrinsic motivation increased. Although this choice was not directly linked to the game itself, it was an effective motivator. Conversely, previous research has reported that contexts in which individuals have no "choice" or "control" can be demotivating (Iyengar & DeVoe, 2003). When people are placed in a situation where they have no control over, they tend to lose motivation for responding and may display anxiety or depression (Seligman, 1975). Thus, lack of choice has been considered to cause detrimental effects on the desire to try the task being assigned.

Botti and Iyengar (2004) sum up the current view of choice as follows:

Decades of research have demonstrated that regardless of whether the choice is trivial, incidental, or even illusory, individuals afforded choice demonstrate more enjoyment and higher task performance in their selected activities, whereas those denied choice experience less intrinsic motivation and decreased psychological and physical well-being (p. 312).

In summary, research findings indicate that choice can be a powerful motivator even when it is trivial or not directly related to the activity itself while no choice can be demotivating.

2.4 Cross-Cultural Views on Autonomy and Choice

Despite the general consensus on the positive influence of "choice" on motivation, some scholars have questioned the universal benefits of the self-determined motivation and autonomy in students' education and learning (Chirkov, 2009; Noels, 2013). According to Markus and Kitayama (2003), autonomy is a socially constructed value, and its meaning is differently negotiated in various socio-culturally contexts. They argue that the construct of autonomy (including cultural values such as individualism, liberalism, independence, self-reliance) are constructions of Western civilization, which are not applicable to the rest of the world, which is less individualistic and more collective or group-oriented. In Western countries, people generally perceive themselves as being separate from others in their environments. They value personal traits that are distinctive and independent of their social roles. As a result, they put more emphasis on autonomy and choice (Sanderson, 2009). In Eastern countries, by contrast, people perceive themselves as being interconnected with and interdependent on others. They value harmony with their social context and make efforts to fit in it. As a result, their behaviors are determined by or contingent upon what they perceive to be the expectations of those who belong to the social community that surrounds them (Markus & Kitayama, 2003). Thus, it is suggested that Easterners find it more motivating to have "significant others" such as their mothers or fathers make a choice for them.

2.5 Studies on Choice

This controversy of choice has been explored by Iyengar and Leeper (1999). They conducted a study to examine the relevance and limitations of choice for cultures in which individuals possess more interdependent models of the self. The participants of their study were 52 Asian American and 53 Anglo American children enrolled in two schools in San Francisco. The children took part in experimental sessions in which they had to work on anagrams under two conditions. In one condition, children themselves chose the puzzles while in another they were told that their mothers chose the puzzles. The results showed that Asian children did best when they worked on the anagrams which they were told that these anagrams had been chosen by their mothers while Anglo Americans did best when they themselves chose the anagrams they worked on.

Iyengar (2010) conducted another study with 100 American and 100 Japanese college students when she stayed in Kyoto, Japan. In the study, she had the participants write all the aspects of their lives in which they like having a choice on one side of a piece of paper and write all the aspects in which they would prefer not to have a choice on the back. The results demonstrated that the Americans' front pages were filled with answers such as "my job," "where I want to live," and "whom I vote for," and the back was almost blank. By contrast, the Japanese students wrote very few items on the front pages while they wrote more on the back. For example, they wrote that they prefer someone else to decide "what they ate," "what they wrote," "when they woke up in the morning," or "what they did at their job." Iyengar (2010) explained the reason for this dependence on others as follows:

[T]he assumption is that your parents, and elders in general, will show the right way to live your life so that you will be protected from making a costly mistake. There are "right" choices and "wrong" ones, and by following elders, you will learn to choose correctly, even relinquish choice when appropriate. (p. 46)

Based on these results, Iyengar (2010) concluded that cultural orientations such as individualistic or collectivistic influence attitudes toward having a choice.

3. Purpose of the Study

The present study is exploratory and situated as the first phase of an ongoing research project that aims at investigating Easterners' perceptions of "choice." To be specific, it explores how Japanese college students perceive choice offered in an English class in Tokyo, Japan.

4. Method
4.1 Participants and Instrument

The participants of the current study were 78 music college students (1st year = 37, 2nd year = 41) who were enrolled in four different English classes taught by the author. Their majors included piano, wind instruments, music education, computer music and music information. They took part in a project titled "Talk like a TED speaker," which consisted of two components: studying selected TED Talks about music and giving a presentation on a topic of their own choice. After the project was completed, the participants' perceptions of the choice were examined using a questionnaire, which included a yes-no question about whether or not the choice motivated them and an open-ended question about how they perceived the choice.

4.2 Project: "Talk Like a TED Speaker"

This project was conducted in four stages. First, three TED Talks were used as teaching materials for studying English, music-related content, and presentation skills. Second, a presentation task titled "Talk like a TED speaker" was assigned. Third, students gave a presentation in the classroom using Google Slides. Finally, their perceptions of choice were collected using a questionnaire. Table 1 briefly outlines these four stages of the project.

Table 1
Project: "Talk like a TED Speaker"

Stage [Weeks]	Descriptions
Stage 1 Studying TED Talks [Week 1~6]	[Goals of the Project] Studying TED Talks on music-related content, students will be able to 1) develop English skills, 2) learn about music-related content, 3) improve presentation skills. [Teaching procedures] Students worked on the following activities with a worksheet: 1) watch the talk with subtitles, 2) answer comprehension questions, 3) discuss the content in groups, and 4) write a summary and reflection as an

69

assignment.
[Teaching materials: TED Talks]
1) "Transformative power of music" by Benjamin Zander
2) "How Frustration can make us more creative" by Tim Hartford
3) "Lead like the great conductor" by Itay Talgam
[Worksheet]
A worksheet for each TED Talk consisted of a vocabulary list, warm-up questions, comprehension questions, and discussion questions.
[Transcript]
Transcripts of each talk were provided.
The Japanese translation was given to those who requested.

Stage 2
Preparation for Presentations
[Week 7~9]

After studying these three talks, students were assigned a 5-minute presentation with a title, "Talk like a TED speaker." They were told that they should choose a topic for themselves and that the topic should be interesting, meaningful, and inspiring for listeners.
[Presentation instruction]
1. "Give a presentation (5 minutes) on any topic you want to talk about like a TED speaker."
2. "The topic is your choice.
"Talk about something you have been thinking about, and you feel you want to share with your classmates. You need to have one thesis statement. Explain your ideas by giving examples, reasons, or citing some sources."
"Choose a topic which listeners will feel worth listening to, learn something new, and find interesting. Offer something they can take home as a "souvenir (おみやげ)."
3. Slides
"Make presentation slides using Google Slides and share the slides with the teacher. Use a computer or a smartphone to make slides."
4. Preparation time: two weeks (one lesson spent in the computer room.

Stage 3
Giving Presentations
[Week 10~11]

In class, students gave a presentation with the slides they made and conducted a Q & A session with the classmates.

Stage 4
Questionnaire
[Week 12]

Students filled out a questionnaire on how they perceived having a choice in choosing their presentation topics and content.
Questionnaire items:

1) Did choosing a presentation topic yourself increase your motivation for the presentation?
2) What do you think about having a choice in choosing your own presentation topic?

5. Results and Discussion

This section reports the results of the project in two sections. The first section describes the topics and titles which students chose for their presentations to illustrate what kind of topics they chose. The second section reports the results of the questionnaire to show how the students perceived the choice in choosing their presentation topics.

5.1 Topics Students Chose

The topics which the participants chose were varied: 28% of them chose to talk about music, 23% about health-related issues, and 15% about how to live their lives more positively. The other topics included pets, culture, education and personal stories (Table 2).

Table 2

Topics Students Chose

Ranking	Genre	n	%
1	Music	22	28%
2	Health	18	23%
3	Wisdom for life	12	15%
4	Animals/Pet	7	9%
5	Culture	4	5%
5	Education	4	5%
5	Personal Story	4	5%
6	Entertainment	2	3%
6	Hometown	2	3%
7	Fashion/Travel/Food	1	1%

Note. N= 78.

Some of the presentation titles about music are shown in Table 3.

Table 3

Titles of the Presentations about Music

Can music heal diseases and mental problems?
Why do we listen to sad love songs when we break up with our boy/girlfriend?
The development of game music and computer technology
Why harp music soothes our minds
How to enjoy orchestra concerts
The crisis of composers
How I composed music with my cats
Stradivarius' fascination
Music with a view: NHK taiga drama's music
How to listen to jazz
The power of ensemble

Some of the titles about the other topics are shown in Table 4.

Table 4

Titles of the Presentations about Other Topics

The meanings of the dreams we have
The nutrients of the kiwifruit for beauty and health
How to live positively
Three effects of stretching
Crying is good for us
The effects of green tea
Why good sleep is important for us
My remedy: tomatoes
How breathing helps us stay healthy
The importance of breakfast
What forgetting brings us
How to keep my apartment clean
What you are looking for is near you
How to survive when we don't have money
What kind of influences do beliefs have on us?
The importance of opening our hearts

Overall, the topics which the students chose were diverse, interesting, and stimulating, reflecting their academic interests and daily lives. Many of them (28%) chose to talk about music-related topics. For example, a music therapy major gave a presentation on "Why do we listen to sad love songs when we break up with our boyfriend?" A computer music major talked about how he composed music using his cats' movements. A jazz major gave a short lecture on the history of jazz and how to listen to jazz. A music composition major talked about his concern over the future of music composers due to the advancement of artificial intelligence. The other students also talked about topics related to their own majors such as performing in an orchestra and playing in an ensemble. The quality of these presentations was equally high, and their classmates' interest in and enthusiasm about the content of the presentations were also high.

The rest of the students (72%) gave a presentation on a variety of topics. Many of the topics were related to how to live a positive, healthy, and happy life. For example, one student demonstrated how to do stretching exercise, and another showed a breathing exercise to improve physical and mental health. One student who lived alone talked about how to keep his apartment clean, and another talked about how he managed to cook dinner every night to save money. The other topics similarly offered helpful suggestions on improving health and mental conditions.

Generally, the topics chosen by the students were original and creative, and it was clear that students tried hard to make their presentations interesting and worth listening to. Although further research is necessary, it might be possible to speculate that this success was due to the fact that the students chose the topics themselves after thinking deeply and carefully about what to talk about. Furthermore, it might be possible to attribute the success to the TED Talks students studied. Because they watched inspiring presentations which offered helpful insights and wisdom, they felt that they wanted to try the same like the speakers.

5.2 Questionnaire Results

The questionnaire administered after the presentation was analyzed using both descriptive statistics and qualitative analysis. The first question asked whether or not the choice in choosing the presentation topic motivated students to try harder. Many students acknowledged the value of having the choice in their classrooms: 41 students (59%) reported that having the choice increased their motivation while 11 students (15%) mentioned that they preferred being given a topic. 19 students (24%) stated that both situations made no difference. Interestingly, seven students (9%) reported that although they were not comfortable with the situation where they had to choose a topic, they changed their minds later and thought that it was better to have a choice. Thus, the choice in this project was positively perceived by more than half of the students.

The second research question asked the reasons for choosing their answers to the first question. Table 5 shows the reasons in the order of the three groups: Group 1: those who supported the choice; Group 2: those who did not support the choice; and Group 3: those who changed their minds.

Table 5

Reasons for the responses

[Group 1: 41 students] Those who preferred having the choice
・自分が決めたトピックのほうが話しやすい。(It is easier to talk about a topic I choose.)
・自分の好きなことについてのほうが、興味を持ってもらえる自信がある。(I am more confident when I talk about a topic I choose.)
・一人ひとり話したいトピックは違うから。(Each person has a different interest.)
・自分で選択したほうが、プレゼンへの興味も高まって、完成度が高まるから。(I will be more interested in getting my presentation ready, and it will be more successful.)

・自分の話しやすい内容を選べたほうが話の幅が広がりやすい。(It will be more fun for each person to choose a topic and we can listen to a variety of content.)
・自分が話したいと思うことをもっと英語で伝えられるようになりたいから。(I want to be able to express what I want to talk about in English.)
・自分で選んだほうがよりやる気になって、話す・話せることがあると思うから。(I will be more motivated to give a presentation.)
・興味のあることについて、深く調べ、英語と同時に他のことも学べるから。(I can research and learn not only English but also what I am interested in.)
・先生に決めてもらうより、トピックを決めるのに少し時間がかかると思うけど、自分が話しやすくなる。(It is easier to talk about what I am interested in although it might take a longer time to prepare.)

[Group 2: 11 students] Those who prefer having the teacher choose the topic
・トピックを決める時間が惜しい。(I don't want to waste time by thinking about what to talk about.)
・トピックを選ぶのは難しい。(It is difficult to choose a topic.)
・話したいトピックがない。(I don't have a topic I want to talk about.)
・自分で選ぶと、範囲が広すぎて考えが分散してしまう。
(It is difficult to narrow down the scope of the topic.)
・私たちはまだよくわからないので先生に任せたい。
(I want my teacher to select a topic for me because we are not ready to do so yet.)
・先生にきめてもらったほうがみんなは等しいから。
(I want my teacher to select a topic because everybody will be in the same condition.)
・自分で決めるとただ楽しさだけで決めてしまって話題を広げられるか不安。
(If I choose a topic, I will choose something fun and probably cannot talk about it extensively.)
・自分で決めると、関心のあるものしかやりませんが、決めていただくことにより新しいことが学べるから。
(If I choose a topic, I will talk only about something I am interested in, but if I am given a topic, I can learn something new.)
・自分でテーマを考えるのは得意ではないので、先生に決めてもらうか、いくつかのテーマの中から選びたい。
(I am not good at choosing a topic, so I want my teacher to give one or give us a list of selected topics.)

[Group 3: 7 students] Those who changed their perceptions of choice
・最初は自分でトピックを選ぶのはいやだったが、プレゼンの準備をしているうちに興味が増して自分でトピックを選んでよかったと思った。
(Although I was not comfortable with choosing a topic, I became engaged in while preparing for my presentation and felt that it was better to have a choice.

・長い間、トピックを決めるのに時間がかかったが、自分の興味のあることだったので、プレゼンを楽しめた。 (It took me a long time to choose a topic, but I enjoyed giving a presentation because I was interested in the topic.)

Note. The English translation is provided by the author.

    As the students' written comments showed, Group 1 supported having the choice in choosing their presentation topic because it allowed them to explore their own interests and to share their own experiences. Furthermore, some felt more confident about giving a presentation because they were able to talk about a topic they knew well. Another merit was that they felt that it was satisfying to know more deeply about a topic they were interested in. For these students, it seems that the choice was a meaningful and effective motivator.

    By contrast, Group 2 stated that they would have been more comfortable if the topic had been given to them by the teacher. As their comments indicated, some felt that they were not able to come up with a topic themselves, or they thought that it would have been much easier if the teacher had given them a topic. One student commented that it was a waste of time to think about what they wanted to talk about. These opinions seem to point to the fact that some Japanese students are not used to choosing a topic themselves and are more comfortable with being told what to do. Although further research is required, it might be possible to argue that some Japanese students are not in the habit of thinking for themselves and feel confused when they are thrust upon a situation where their independent thinking is required. Although it is not conclusive, the students in this group seem to partially support Iyengar's claim (2010) that Easterners do not perform best when they had to choose for themselves.

    Group 3 was noteworthy because they changed their minds while preparing for the presentation. It might be possible to speculate that despite the difficulty in choosing a topic at the initial stage, they became more engaged as they researched and gained more knowledge about the topic and felt that having chosen their own topic was a rewarding, positive experience. This result seems to indicate that if students can find a topic which they enjoy exploring or learning more about, choice has a positive and lasting effect on their motivation.

6. Conclusion

The present study explored Japanese college students' perceptions of choice by conducting a project, which included having students watch TED Talks about music and give presentations after choosing a presentation topic. One of the major findings of the study suggested that many students perceived the choice positively and the choice, in turn, led to increased originality and creativity in the quality of the presentations. Furthermore, having the choice resulted in increased interest in and motivation for giving a presentation.

However, it is important to note that some students were reluctant to be placed in a situation where they had to choose because they felt that they were not able to cope with the situation well. This result seems to partially support some scholars' claim that choice can be a demotivator in a collectivistic society such as Japan (Iyengar, 2010) because many students are not used to making a choice themselves.

Another noteworthy finding is the fact that although some students had negative perceptions of choice initially, they felt more positive about it as they engaged in the presentation. Although further research is necessary, this result seems to indicate that students' perceptions of choice can change, depending on the experience they have. If they have positive, rewarding experiences by making a choice themselves, they may begin to feel positive about choice. Perhaps, they need further practices and experiences to feel more confident about choosing on their own.

In summary, although far from conclusive, these results above seem to indicate that Japanese students' perceptions of choice are varied and that they can be influenced by the experiences they undergo in classrooms. Further research is required, acknowledging the limitations of the current study such as the research design and method.

References

Botti, S. & Iyengar, S. S. (2004). The Psychological Pleasure and Pain of Choosing: When People Prefer Choosing at the Cost of Subsequent Outcome Satisfaction. *Journal of Personality and Social Psychology, 87*, 312-326.

Chirkov, V. I. (2009). A self-determination theory perspective. *Theory and Research in Education, 7*(2), 253-262.

Cordova, D. I., & Lepper, M. R. (1996). Intrinsic motivation and the process of learning: Beneficial effects of contextualization, personalization, and choice. *Journal of Educational Psychology, 88*(4), 715-730.

Deci, E. L. & Ryan, R. M. (1985). *Intrinsic Motivation and Self-determination in Human Behavior.* New York: Plenum.

Deci, E. L., Eghrari, H., Patrick, B. C., & Leone, D. R. (1994). Facilitating internalization: The self-determination theory perspective. *Journal of Personality, 62*, 119–142.

Deci, E. L., & Ryan, R. M. (2008). Self-determination theory: A macrotheory of human motivation, development, and health. *Canadian Psychology/Psychologie Canadienne, 49*(3), 182-185.

Deci, E. L., Vallerand, R. J., Pelletier, L. G., & Ryan, R. M. (1991). Motivation and education: The self-determination perspective. *Educational Psychologist, 26*(3-4), 325-346.

Flowerday, T., & Schraw, G. (2000). Teachers' beliefs about instructional choice: A phenomenological study. *Journal of Educational Psychology, 92*, 634-645.

Iyengar, S. S. (2010). *The art of choosing.* New York: Grand Central Publishing.

Iyengar, S. S., & DeVoe, S. E. (2003). Rethinking the value of choice: Considering cultural mediators of intrinsic motivation. In V. Murphy-Berman & J. J. Berman (Eds.). *Nebraska Symposium on Motivation: Cross-cultural differences in perspectives on the self* (Vol. 49, pp. 129-174). Lincoln: University of Nebraska Press.

Iyengar, S. S., & Leeper, M. R. (1999). Rethinking the value of choice: A cultural perspective on intrinsic motivation. *Journal of Personality and Social Psychology, 76*(3), 349-366.

Markus, H. R., & Kitayama, S. (2003). Models of agency: Sociocultural diversity in the construction of action. In V. Murphy-Berman & J. J. Berman (Eds.). *Nebraska Symposium on Motivation: Cross-cultural differences in perspectives on the self* (Vol. 49, pp. 1-57). Lincoln: University of Nebraska Press.

Niemiec, C. P., & Ryan, R. M. (2009). Applying self-determination theory to educational practice. *Theory and Research in Education, 7*(2), 133-144.

Noels, K.A. (2013). Learning Japanese; learning English: Promoting motivation through autonomy, competence, and relatedness. In Apple, M., Da Silva, D. & T. Fellner (eds.) *Language Learning Motivation in Japan* (pp. 15-34). Bristol, UK: Multilingual Matters.

Noels, K. A., Pelletier, L.G., Clement, R. & Vallerand, R. J. (2000). Why are you learning a second language? Motivational orientations and self-determination theory. *Language Learning, 53*, 33-63.

Rotter, J. B. (1966). Generalized expectancies for internal versus external control of reinforcement. *Psychological Monographs, 80*, 1-28.

Ryan, R. M., & Deci, E. L. (2000). Intrinsic and extrinsic motivations: Classic definitions and new directions. *Contemporary Educational Psychology, 25*, 54-67.

Ryan, R. M., & Deci, E. L. (2000). Self-determination theory and the facilitation of intrinsic motivation, social development, and well-being. *American Psychologist, 55*, 68-78.

Sanderson, C.A. (2009). *Social Psychology*. New York: John Wiley & Sons.

Seligman, M. E. P. (1975). *Helplessness: On depression, development, and death*. San Francisco: W. H. Freeman.

Taylor, S. E. (1989). *Positive illusions: Creative self-deception and the healthy mind.* New York: Basic Books.

Zuckerman, M., Porac, J., Lathin, D., Smith, R., & Deci, E. L. (1978). On the importance of self-determination for intrinsically motivated behavior. *Personality and Social Psychology Bulletin, 4*, 443-446.

［本論文は *Journal of Language Learner Development,* Vol. 1 (2018)に発表した論文に加筆したものです。］

索　引

【あ】
絵本　44
オーセンティックな教材　3, 5, 8
【か】
外的　3, 4, 5
外発的　3, 4
関係性　3, 4
教科学習　30
言語学習　30, 44
【さ】
自己決定理論　3, 4, 5, 8
児童文学　44
自律性　3, 4, 7
自律的な学び　6
【た】
チョイス　1, 59
同一化　4, 5
動機づけ　3, 4, 5
質問　5
統合的　5, 30
取り入れ的　4
【な】
内発的　3, 4, 5, 6, 8
内容重視教授法　8
【ま】
モチベーション　3, 6, 30, 44, 59
【や】
有能性　3, 4

【A】
adult education 45
authentic materials 27, 32, 33
autonomy 62, 63, 64, 65
【C】
children's literature 48, 49, 50, 51
choice 11, 59, 60, 63, 64, 65, 66, 67
cognitive evaluation theory 12, 61
collectivistic 66, 75
competence 62, 77
content and language integrated instruction 14, 30
content-based instruction 30, 33, 39
【E】
English learning motivation questionnaire 18
expectancy-value theory 10
external regulation 18
extrinsic motivation 12, 13, 14
【I】
identified regulation 18, 23
individualistic 65, 66
instrumental orientation 10
integrated regulation 14
integrative orientation 10
intrinsic motivation 11, 12, 14, 16, 17, 63
introjected regulation 13, 18

【L】
L2 readers 48
literary competence 45
【M】
motivation 18, 19, 22, 23, 24
【O】
organismic integration theory 12
【P】
panel study 17
picture books 44, 45, 46, 48, 50, 52, 56, 57, 62, 77
【R】
relatedness 62, 77
【S】
second language (L2) /foreign language (FL) reading 45
self-determination theory 19, 10, 14, 16, 18, 60, 62
【T】
TED Talks 6, 8, 17, 19, 20, 21, 22, 24, 25, 68, 71

著者略歴

林　千代（はやし　ちよ）

現職：国立音楽大学音楽学部　教授
略歴：イースタンミシガン大学英米文学学部修士課程修了。テンプル大学教育学部応用言語学博士課程修了。国際基督教大学専任講師を経て、現職。
専門：応用言語学、英語教育学（特に学習者要因に関する研究）

Chiyo Hayashi, Ed. D

Professor at Kunitachi College of Music
Master of Arts from Eastern Michigan University (Major: English and American Literature)
Doctor of Education from Temple University (Major: Applied Linguistics)
Research Interests: Individual differences in learning a second language (motivation and beliefs, pronunciation, and curriculum development)

Motivating EFL Learners with Authentic Materials
英語学習者のモチベーションを高めるための授業実践とその効果
―オーセンティックな教材を用いて―

平成 31 年 3 月 25 日　発行

著　者　林　千代
発行所　株式会社　溪水社
　　　　広島市中区小町 1-4（〒730-0041）
　　　　電　話（082）246-7909／FAX（082）246-7876
　　　　e-mail:info@keisui.co.jp

ISBN978-4-86327-475-4　C3082